The Sky Is My Witness

Thomas Moore

THE SKY IS MY WITNESS

The Sky

Is My Witness

By Captain THOMAS MOORE, JR., U.S.M.C.R

G·P·PUTNAM'S SONS

NEW YORK

In the main, this is the story of myself and others like me—all commissioned Marine pilots. But not all the people connected with flying planes are officers. Quite a number of our best pilots are enlisted men, and practically *all* those who make the pilot's job at all possible —those who service the planes, patch them together again, see to it that everything still works and keeps working—these are enlisted men. Perhaps this isn't orthodox, but it is my sincere belief that these constitute the substance to our shadow. Let's put it this way—we officer pilots do a hell of a lot that people hear about— officer pilots being more or less the glamor boys—but the enlisted of aviation do one hell of a lot that very few people hear about. It is to these enlisted of aviation that I humbly dedicate this book.

T. M., Jr.

I want to take this opportunity to thank E. Ralph Emmett for his help in the preparation of this book.

Contents

THE SKY IS MY WITNESS

1. *Intermission*

When I returned, I thought:

It's over now for me. I don't know for how long, but for now—right now—it's over. Pearl Harbor, Midway, the Hebrides, Guadalcanal—places and names on newspaper maps. I'll read them, cluck my tongue, and forget them fast like everyone else. I'll sleep well. No more dreams, and, while my wounds are healing, I will heal too. I will lose myself in my family, my friends, and in laughter. I'll laugh louder than anything. I'll laugh so loud I'll hear nothing, remember nothing. It's a long journey passed between me and the war. I'm beyond it now. Completely. I'm going to fill these days so full that I never ever will have time to recall those other days. Never ever!

Yeah?

Came the questioning people. Everywhere I went there was one. The last time was last night. The last ten times were last night. It is morning now, but when I go out, they will be there again. The last one, last night, was typical. I don't know his name. They seldom offer it. They offer cigars. This one would offer cigars; he had rows of them in the pockets of his vest, and a diamond ring. He poked the diamonded finger at my battle ribbons; that was his self-introduction.

"You been overseas?"

"Yes." Remember, be pleasant. Be pleasant.

"See any action?" He hoped.

When I was not quick to answer—

"Where? Have a cigar."

That was how it was. Have a cigar, blow smoke rings with a stranger, and tell him, between each puff, how you killed a lot of other strangers, how you remembered pictures when you thought you'd die, how you felt deep inside when your best friends went down burning. Tell him all those things while blowing smoke rings. Tell him so he can tell an "inside" story that will entertain his guests for a few moments at tomorrow's luncheon.

It was not yesterday that I decided to tell this story. It was a long time ago. By a long time I mean a month. It was soon after I returned home, when the first glorious thrill of homecoming had passed, when the questioning began, and when I began to dream again.

I could not halt them. In the tranquil aura of a church some familiar organ chord would set them off, and instead of a hymnal I would hear drums. Or when I was among old friends and a phrase was spoken that belonged to other voices, a phrase that my memory would respond to as to a bugle, then I would remember and go on remembering for hours without end.

I tried to forget it all. I tried hard. If I had wanted to rid myself of the memory of my own name, it would have been easier. Then, sometimes, often, I remembered the Ancient Mariner, who had told his tale that he might be free of it; but every time such a thought came to me I dispelled it. Already too many mariners were telling too many tales. But The Mariner seemed to walk beside me always, repeating and repeating the reason why he had given his account. If I argued that I was not a hero, I was reminded that neither was he.

When I did finally decide to tell this story, I found

4

there was a shortage of listeners. Oh yes, there were plenty of people who would hear me—people like the one last night, parades of them. But I wanted a listener who would hear me and understand what I meant and heed the meaning of what I said. Of such listeners, I could think of few.

Monsignor Daniel McCarthy would have been the first to whom I would have come.

I was at the U. S. Naval Hospital in Brooklyn when I thought of him. For several days I had been confined for clinical treatment of injuries received in the Solomons action. On one of those days I was reading a newspaper, and then somehow I thought of Sunday. Sunday, I knew, I would go to church as usual. It would be pleasant to go back to the old parish and hear the Mass as I used to before the war—as Monsignor McCarthy pronounced it.

He would be the one. He would understand. He would guide me now as he had guided me to say the catechism. I would answer now as to another catechism, confidently and completely. He had only to begin to ask. Sunday I would speak to him.

Then—coincidence of coincidences!—no sooner had I pronounced my thoughts when I was informed that a visitor was waiting to see me. "He's some kind of chaplain," the orderly explained. And it was Monsignor McCarthy who had come, Monsignor McCarthy, stanch keeper of the faith at St. Mark's Church in Brooklyn. He knew me long and he knew me well. As I remembered and pictured him, his hair had been gray; it had become white now, adding to his calm, ecclesiastical appearance.

We shook hands, and he said, "I'm glad to see you home again, Tom."

I returned the greeting, adding, with conviction, "And I'm glad to see *you* again, Monsignor."

He sat down at a chair beside my bed, and I started to say something. But he began. He handed me a carton of Camels. I was about to thank him for the cigarettes, when he gave me something else—a rosary.

I should have said more than only, "Thank you." I wanted to tell him how grateful I was for his sentiment, but I didn't know how to say it without sounding awkward. The rosary beads my mother had given me ten years before are still on Guadalcanal.

Then he said, "Well, Tom, from what I hear it was only by the grace of God that you've come back to us."

I fully agreed. "Yes, Monsignor, that's true." I wound the rosary around my fingers, trying to compose words of beginning, and hoping that he would say them first.

"And did you go to confession and receive Communion while you were away, Tom?"

Perhaps it would be the best way—to begin on a religious trend. "Yes, Monsignor," I replied, "I went to services and—" And I told him accounts of how, in spite of the hardships and dangers, the chaplains of all faiths carried on their services to give us consolation no matter where we were. Then, as I talked with the good Monsignor, telling him of the things that would make him happiest, I gradually realized that he was not the one to hear me. I knew that what I wished to say was not to be kept under vows of silence.

Monsignor Daniel McCarthy was a man of peace, good will, and the brotherhood of man. He was divorced from conflict as all clerics are so divorced. And here was I, Thomas Moore, with the mark of battle more in accent on my words than in the scars upon my face. It was incongruous that *any* one man alone should be my listener....

For now I knew I must speak to all men of good will—and that is a polite name for some of them—who have so remained even in these days. I must try to tell them how I and others like me—there are many—may change to men of ill will upon our homecoming, and how we reason through the eternity before that homecoming.

And that is why all this is told.

2. The Civil Life

It is said that every story must have a beginning and an end, but at this writing the end is still beyond me. Indeed, until this war is won there will be no end for me—not so long as I still can fly with bombs beneath my wings.

Yet, today I think of the end—my end. I think of it because today is a day of inactivity, and I have time to think. But in the long run, it will be simple. It will be as Alan Seeger, the soldier-poet, wrote before Verdun:

> *It may be he shall take my hand*
> *And lead me into his dark land*
> *And close my eyes and quench my breath—*
> *It may be I shall pass him still.* *

Now and again I think of those words; in truth, I am never unaware of them. Always they keep pounding upon my ears in the voices of gremlins, taunting, questioning—*the end? The end?* . . .

This is the beginning.

I am the second son of Thomas and Cecilia Moore—Irish-Americans, middle-class, Catholics. I was born on July 14, 1917, in New York City—in the few acres of the city bordering on Hell's Kitchen.

Hell's Kitchen . . . the name fitted it well. I must say something of that place. It is part of my background; it is where I spent the first impressionable years of my life, and those impressions have ever remained strong.

---

* From *Poems by Alan Seeger*. Copyright, 1916, Charles Scribner's Sons.

It was a place where the normal pursuit of happiness was forbidden by ordinances that were crowded one upon the other. If there was some sparse plot of grass within a mile or two, its virginity was protected by the sign *Don't Walk*. If there was a blank wall from which a handball could bounce, it, too, was inviolable. *No Ball Playing, No Loitering, No Noise*—no anything! And if these signs could be escaped and nullified in our minds, and some stolen hours in a vacant lot be had, then *Fletcher's Castoria—Babies Cry for It, Coca-Cola—It's Refreshing, I'd Walk a Mile for a Camel*—these huge billboards would be the horizon, north, east, south, and west.

The granite squares of sidewalk were our good earth, and its slim boundaries were always contested. We fought then for *Lebensraum* in the shape of things like a gutter in which to play marbles, stickball, or roller-skate hockey. If you wanted more space, you could stand on your ear and whistle for it—and keep whistling; I think it was there I first began to dream of flying.

When I was six, I went off to a big red schoolhouse, wearing a clean white shirt and a bright red tie. There began the making of this American.

I learned to read and to write and to add fractions together. Later, twenty years later, I used the reading I had learned to read weather reports; I used the writing lessons in composing my reports: "...Dived upon carrier, released bomb..."; I added fractions together to chart my path, one among thousands, across the pages of tomorrow's history primers.

I see us as we were, a thousand loud-mouthed Flanagans, Torrellis, Schmidts, Ginsburgs, Fenwicks clashing daily on the crowded streets, and then, the next morning, standing suddenly quiet and attentive in our

9

American schoolhouse by the Ninth Avenue El, reciting in soprano-like voices the honored oath of allegiance: "... to the flag ... the United States of America ... the Republic ... One nation, indivisible ... liberty and justice for all."

Flanagan, Torrelli, Schmidt, Ginsburg, Fenwick. P. S. 17 may well be proud of those names. Some lie buried in places that their geography lessons never even mentioned.

My father had become a policeman, and after diligent saving he made a down payment on a house in the Sheepshead Bay section of Brooklyn. This was a tremendous move not alone in location but also in prestige. In becoming free of Tenth Avenue, we became "propertied Irish." Though the bank did actually own our entire house except for a few bricks, we were property owners. One must have lived on Tenth Avenue to appreciate the music in those words.

There, on Avenue Y, beside Sheepshead Bay, the Moore family flourished. My brother Jack, my sisters Margaret and Roberta, and I were joined by an additional sister, Patricia. And, as in every family where the needs are modest and the income regular, things were good.

In the four years from 1930 to 1934 I attended Abraham Lincoln High School, graduating in June. I can recall little of those days. It was just a time of pimples, blushes, and confusion. When I graduated, in addition to my diploma I took with me several scholarship scrolls, which were promptly framed, a pin of membership in Arista, the scholastic honor society, and a desire to enter Annapolis.

I never got to Annapolis. Perhaps it is just as well. It sounded big and important at the time—especially the picture of myself in a midshipman's uniform parading informally up Broadway. Arrangements had almost been made for me to enter Manhattan College when my father arrived home one day from work with the story of how another policeman's son had transferred his enthusiasm for Annapolis to the New York State Merchant Marine Academy. I was still seventeen, and here again were brass buttons. Of course I wanted to go!

So for two years, from 1934 to 1936, I attended the academy and wore a uniform and absorbed my quota of the many subjects with which an officer of the Merchant Marine must have an acquaintance. There were times, however, when the sound of motors overhead caused me to wonder why I was preparing myself for the career of a sailor.

Upon completion of the two-year course, I was awarded the license to act as third mate on ships of unlimited tonnage on any ocean, becoming at nineteen one of the youngest qualified third mates in the country. I was impressed, but not so the shipowners. There were too many sailors, too many third mates, and too few ships. So I ceased looking to the sea. It was a friendly place, but it was 1936, I needed a job, and the sea was not encouraging.

Then suddenly I did find a job, a sea job—or almost a sea job. I was given the captaincy of a 65-foot vessel that plied the waters of Long Island Sound, loaded to the gunwales with amateur fishermen. Every day for those two summer months, I guided my ship on the voyage out to the fishing grounds. It was a good job. It was good to cry out such terms as "Drop the hook" ... "Stand by your helm!" ... "Let go the starboard line!" ... "Steady! Steady as she goes!" ... But all too soon came fall and reality.

11

I was again just a twenty year old looking for a job. It was 1937, and that meant any job. I found it in the studios of Dave Fleischer, the producer of animated cartoons and one of my fishing-boat passengers. I was hired to color pictures of such personalities as Popeye and Betty Boop. It was an unusual occupation, but it was occupying. Seventeen dollars a week, and a little dark-haired artist named Janet for company.

Janet became my girl. When I kissed her for the first time, it was still 1937—September, I think. Perhaps I should have been conscious of important things then. Things like Spain fighting for her life. And China. But we were far away from those guns and those people. *We're Americans.* The words alone sounded protective enough. Fight your own battles, I reasoned with no reason at all. So I kissed Janet again, or shut my ears, or turned the radio louder when anyone mentioned them.

Then came 1938. The Fleischer studios were moved to Miami and Janet decided to go with them. I intended to look for another job in New York as I wanted to take the forthcoming Civil Service Examination for the New York City Police Force. However, the examination was postponed indefinitely, and I decided to go to Florida after all. The nights there were wide and starry, wonderful to walk by, ecstatic when Janet walked beside me. It was 1938, and the *Journal* cried out some words about a man named Hitler, and Chamberlain, and a city called Prague; the guns were still pounding in Spain and China, and on the borders all over the world new guns were being moved into position. All these momentous things were happening and still I turned the music louder and shut my eyes to the future.

The future—the war—began in 1939. I never let myself listen, even then. There were too many other things to hear, like Janet's voice, a popular tune, the sound of propellers beating in the sky.

I had been spending many hours at the Miami Municipal Airport. At first it was just the sight of the airplanes close up that brought me there. I watched them from behind the netted wire fence, as I used to study the toys behind Macy's Christmas window.

It was satisfying for a while, but then it wasn't. I wanted more. I wanted to go out on the field like those others, the wind-burned, helmeted others who took the planes up to the sky. Up there a man could turn cartwheels. He could lose all inhibitions witnessed by the world. A man could really make himself known up there.

I began to spend many one-dollar bills for minutes in the air. That first one dollar had done it. When I went up for the first time and experienced that iota of a moment when we became air borne, I surrendered to flight forever. It was like a habit-forming drug. I wanted to fly as I had never wanted anything before in my life.

It was the now ominous developments of the faraway war that brought me my chance. When the need for great numbers of pilots was announced by President Roosevelt, his message brought about an expansion of the Civilian Training Program of the CAA to include applicants beyond a college campus. I applied and after several long weeks of waiting the mailman dropped a long, officially unstamped envelope into my postbox. The letter within notified me that I had been accepted as a qualified candidate and set a near date for the start of my training.

If the days of shaving a block of balsa wood into the

image of a thing that flies were the overture, if the days of dreaming and wishing and watching through a netted wire fence were the prelude, if the minutes of flight bought with single dollar bills were the climax—then this opportunity was the triumphant finale to all those days!

I began my lessons with confidence born of this fervor. It was a confidence that manifested itself from the moment I fitted myself into the rear seat of the Piper Club trainer to begin the first of a series of hourly lessons.

Three flying hours later, my confidence turned to a spirit of damned-if-I-won't! resolution. It was a change brought about by the tone of my instructor's voice, which had lost its tolerant, guiding quality. It was acid now, and I cursed him silently but fluently every time we went aloft.

"Where the hell is your co-ordination?" he would shout into my earphones.

"Go climb a donkey's rear end," I would reply without letting a word of it be audible. "Climb it and stay climbed!"

After the first six or seven hours, some of the students were allowed to solo. They went gloriously up alone, and when they came down they were heroes. They laughed and pounded each other, playing down their abilities in the usual phrases of modesty. I didn't blame them a bit. I was simply jealous.

When still more hours had passed, and more of them had been given the go-ahead signal to take off alone, I was still flying like a dunce. It became maddening to watch them. I felt like a penguin in the midst of eagles. I wanted to solo; I felt sure that I could, and my hours of grace were fast ticking to an end.

It was the end of the tenth hour. We were coming in to land, and when we landed the last moment of instruction would be over. Today I would solo. He had to let me solo. If only I was unshackled from this asinine baboon, I felt sure I could fly from here to kingdom come and back again. Then we landed. I didn't solo. I was washed out. "Unfit to fly," they said. "Too dangerous."

I have remembered those words. When things are tense, they make me laugh and feel more easy. But my disappointment then was bitter. They were wrong; they had to be wrong—come hell or high water, I was going to fly!

If war is hell, then hell was on its way. Those few who were far visioned enough to see it decided to prepare for it. They started with the Selective Service Act of 1940. A short time later, the national registration date was set by the Army. But before that date arrived, I was notified by a circular through the mails that the Navy was accepting men with my qualifications for training as pilots.

The circular described, "A colorful, adventurous life awaits the men who take advantage of this great opportunity." It was a well-composed pamphlet. The more times I read it, the more convincing it was. I thought it over for a long time. The words "patriotism," "service," "wings," "salary," "adventure," and "flying" went round and round in my head. This had to be *my* decision. I didn't want to be influenced by anyone; no matter what happened I wanted to blame only myself.

The man behind the desk sorted my papers and found them to be in order.

"You sign here," he said, "alongside the X."

I took the forms and was about to sign when suddenly I noticed for the first time the words at the top:
"*United States Marine Corps Reserve.*"

I started to my feet. "But," I said, "I came here to
join the Navy. This application is for the Marines."

"Sign," the man said. "I saw you first, and you're going to be a marine."

I looked at the man's face. He grinned; I grinned, and
I did what the man said. I signed and became a marine.
I've never regretted the choice.

3. *Military Metamorphosis*

.

I have "The Log" before me as I tell this. "The Log" is a cheap notebook that I bought on the night before I reported for duty as a marine. It is a diary record of all the days I spent in learning to fly and fight. That which follows *is* taken from "The Log."

* * *

January 15, 1941: Today, at ten o'clock in the morning, I bade farewell to civilian life. When I arrived here at Opalocka, Florida, I wore my light gray suit, a white shirt, and a blue tie. I suppose I ought to remember those details, because, if I don't flunk out, it ought to be a long time before I wear such things again.

About sixty other recruits arrived here with me . . . most of them are Navy boys, but we train together . . . Dave Andre Harvie Duval, Bill Moore are here too. They seem to be regular guys, and I suppose we'll become good friends, especially since we're the only Marines in the entire class. The friendly petty jealousies have already started. We're only four against some sixty Navy men, but we're holding our own. Dave, Bill and Harvie have already completed primary and secondary CAA and these three are really grooming me. I should have over a thousand bunk room hours by the end of the month. About the only subject that occupies us is: fly, fly, fly. And the word is we begin tomorrow!

January 16, 1941: All hands reported for a lecture on

17

"Respect." It was given by C.P.O. McCarthy. He's a real old salt. It seems that respect is about the toughest thing in the world for college men to learn. But McCarthy is the man for the teaching. "You're being trained as officers!" he bellows. "Fighting officers! You know what those words mean?"

January 17, 1941: This morning we received part of our uniforms. My light gray suit and all my other clothes are now in a bundle on its way to New York. Sort of symbolic of something, I suppose. . . .

But the most important thing, the really important thing is: Today we began to fly!

I was included in the group of four assigned to a Marine aviator, Lieutenant George Waldie, for instruction. He took each of us aside for a short interview before the hop, and when it was my turn to introduce myself he recognized my New York accent as though every word was a signpost from Times Square. He told me that, since the other fellows had all soloed before, he considered me his first student, because this was his first assignment as an instructor. I think we're going to get along fine—after all, he's from Staten Island.

January 20, 1941: . . . It's become nerve-racking. I don't know what's wrong. Dammit, I know I can fly!— but I'm not making the progress I should. Waldie's a hell of a good guy, but he's becoming a little disgusted, and I can't blame him.

January 24, 1941: I think everything is going to be all right now. Waldie is aces—four of them! Today he proved it. Day after day I've been making my landings

18

with that same old trouble, left wing higher than the right. Well, today this is what happened:

We were making pass after pass at the field with Waldie always yelling, "Keep your wings level on the horizon! Level! Keep your wings level!" Then he told me to try it.

I was nervous as a cat as I started down. I wanted to do this one right, just so Waldie would stop shouting so damn much. We came over the field; I executed a 180 degree turn into the wind and started easing off the throttle. I was doing everything just as he had taught me. I glanced at my altimeter; we were losing just the right amount of altitude. I glanced at the speed indicator; it, too, showed the right answer. Everything was on schedule, just right.

Just as the wheels were about to touch the ground, it happened. The right wing drooped! Waldie grabbed away the controls, poured on the coal, and we roared up again averting a crash landing. I said nothing to Waldie and Waldie said nothing to me as he brought the plane down with a very correct landing.

We taxied to a stop before one of the hangars, and Waldie got out, still silent. Not wanting to get in his way, I planned to remain in the plane until he was out of sight. He walked to the wire fence that borders the field. For a full minute he just stood there, gripping the straps of his parachute, looking to the left, the right, up, and down as though searching for his lost temper. Then he started back. He climbed up on the wing and leaned his arm against the rim of my cockpit.

"Look, Tom," he said in a tired, dispirited voice, "I'm your friend. I like you. I mean it. But for gosh sakes, please keep your wings *level!* Please, do me a favor. Keep them level."

19

So everything is going to be all right. As long as Waldie and I are friends, I can't be nervous any more. It figures.

January 26, 1941: Today is Sunday. I drove down to Miami and spent the day with Janet. . . .

January 28, 1941: This morning I did it! Waldie climbed out and said I could. They tied the long red ribbons to the struts of the wings, and I did it! I went up alone. I soloed!

January 30, 1941: One of the boys had an accident . . . a bad crash. He was killed.

March 3, 1941: I still haven't done any more flying since soloing. I feel like the fellow who's been kissed once and then had the girl shut the door in his face. Waldie has been letting me make a few flights with him, but it isn't like going up alone.

March 27, 1941: Another uneventful day. Exercise and manual of arms is the routine. Each day gets longer than the one before. There's nothing to do but wait, wait, wait; maybe someday someone will remember to send us to Pensacola. The heart games have become cutthroat affairs. We only play for one cent a point, but it seems as though I'll have to become a Philadelphia lawyer to come out on top. When I do, the score sheet is mysteriously lost. Today I made a new rule. Everyone keeps their own score sheet and we check after every game. I'm keeping mine on my khaki trousers, and they'll have to take my pants to beat me. Sometimes I'm afraid they will.

April 15, 1941: Still waiting. Nothing else to write that hasn't been written, rewritten, and re-rewritten.

May 1, 1941: Pensacola here we come—
Right back where we started from!

May 3, 1941: Now we're going to begin and in a big way. Pensacola is everything I ever heard about it and a million things more. The only drawback is that we don't fly or even go near an airplane for six weeks. We start right off on an intensive ground school course.

May 12, 1941: Bill Norval and I had quite a debate tonight about the war. He seems to think it is only a question of time before we go to war . . .
"With Germany?" I asked.
"No," he said, "with Japan!"
So for about an hour we kept arguing, and arguing, and he kept telling me of the things he read and saying that we weren't awake to the Japanese threat. I'm not much along on international politics, but I haven't heard much discord about our relations with the Japs. We're still selling her war material, while we've just about gone every-way short of an A.E.F. against the Nazis. I'm putting all this down because Bill said that the events in the future are going to make me eat my words. Maybe so. Time will tell.

July 7, 1941: I'm getting along fairly well. We've had quite a bit of primary work and some acrobatics. It's become quite a gag now for the rest of the boys in the primary training squadron. They say, "Tom Moore is up on an acrobatic hop. Get the bucket and swab ready." I'd get sick and flash my hash on every acrobatic hop.

While I was sick I'd want to get back on the ground quick, but when I got down I could hardly wait to go up and get sick again.

Soon we begin formation, instrument, and night flying. Also we'll start using faster and more advanced ships. Now that I've turned acrobatics in the air, I'm beginning to call myself half a flyer. We're all pretty cocky, because the hardest haul is over. I wish the folks at home could have seen me when I executed that sharp snap-roll this morning. In fact, I'd like to give them a show some time over the house in Brooklyn just to convince them that I can really fly. . . .

September 8, 1941: Bill and I had another one of those debates on the war. He says that the Japs would fight us if they thought they had any kind of chance to win. They'd fight to end the Open Door policy in the Far East. I still think he's got bells in his head. If we're going to fight, we'll fight with Germany. If the Russians don't fold up, as they probably will, we can all jump Hitler through France and end the whole business damned fast. But right now it looks as if Moscow will soon fall, and I suppose the Russians will pull out like the French.

September 29, 1941: Well, our course here at Pensacola is just about ended, and from here we move to Miami. Hot dog!

September 30, 1941: We leave for Miami any day now. . . .

November 4, 1941: I have just made a night flight over Miami. Lord, it was wonderful! You can write poems about the feelings you get flying high over a lighted city. We took off, and when we were flying free and clear I looked back. The runway was like a road that ran between two rows of burning torches. Above me the stars were like millions of diamonds on a black velvet tray. Near me the others flew; we kept formation by marking the orange bullets that spit from the next man's exhaust. I felt as if we were charging horsemen racing over the city, and everyone below must have heard us.

It is difficult to imagine that the flight was to practice night attacks. Somehow the word "attack" didn't enter my mind or fit into the picture. I wonder if I will ever fit tonight's flight into use against an enemy. After all, isn't that the purpose to all we've been doing?...

November 17, 1941: I had better begin to make arrangements with a tailor for my officer's uniform. Already I've sat for my portrait photograph to be put into the *Flight Jacket*—our yearbook. In a few more weeks: graduation.

The word is that we'll all be made instructors upon graduation, because of the great influx of new men, but it's only the word—and the word is more often wrong than right.

November 28, 1941: ... There is more and more talk about Japan, especially among the officers who have been on duty at Pacific stations. They really look at war objectively. I suppose that's the sign of a professional officer.

December 3, 1941: We are finishing up our necessary flying hours. Graduation is coming closer and closer.

Today I bought my gold wings, but until the last moment they remain in the box, nice and shiny. A lot of the boys are paying close attention to the radio now that things are what they are with Japan. But right here and now, I still say that we won't fight—not that anyone says we will. The word "war" doesn't seem to ring very true when I mention it in connection with the United States.... My new uniform fits well, and I look rather sharp in it, if I do say so myself.

December 7, 1941: It's come. War. We're at war. The United States is at War. The Japanese attacked Pearl Harbor this morning. It didn't hit me at first, not the full meaning. We—Janet and I—were sitting in a restaurant talking to a musician when it was announced on the radio. The first words I said were, "Well, there goes my graduation leave." Just that.

But tonight I feel different. I feel sort of little, but I also feel purposeful. Some of the fellows were running around blowing off more steam than would take to run a train from here to Tokyo, but we're all pretty quiet now. We all know what we've got to do. We've got to win this war....

December 9, 1941: Today was graduation. There was not much of a fuss. We twelve graduating pilots just took off for the last time as students on a practice bombing flight. When we came down, Commander Bogan handed us our commissions in his office, and when we went outside we pinned on our wings and shoulder bars, and shook hands all around. The uncertainty of waiting for orders has been keeping us all on edge. I saw Bill Norval's on the desk in our room before he did and attached a note, "Peoria Flash going to beautiful Pacific." He got mine first and wrote, "Dodgers off for Tokyo."

My orders provide for twenty-three days' leave, including travel time; after that I am to report to the Advanced Carrier Training Group at San Diego, California. California, here I come!

*　　*　　*

Here "The Log" ends.

I went back to Sheepshead Bay to spend my leave with the family. It was great to see them again and we had a wonderful time together telling each other the thousands of stories that had piled up since I had been away. I was treated like a royal guest, and I enjoyed every minute of it. We forgot about the war for the moment—or we made each other think so, anyway.

Then, when my leave came to an end, and I was ready to leave for Grand Central Station, we had our little scene.... Like every father, my father, also, solemnly shook my hand. And like every mother, my mother kissed me and brushed away her tears with her familiar blue-bordered apron.

4. *Janet Is My Wife*

Janet is my wife. My wife. . . . It is only lately, since my return from Guadalcanal, that the meaning of these words has come through to me. It is in these interluding days between what the past has been and what the future will be that I have come to know her deeply and to recognize how very dependent I am upon her. By day it is Janet, little Janet, who plans our world for my son and me. And by night it is Janet again, who with her words and arms guides us back when we cry out from sleep.

We have a past, Janet and I, the simple, treasured past that evolves about any two people whose love has weathered a test of time. For five years it ran, a past of ice-skating and dances, petty arguments and wonderful episodes of forgiveness. Someday soon we'd marry. We'd have a house, our house. We'd have children. It was only a matter of getting settled in something secure, that's all. An old story.

But when war came and my orders came, I thought differently. The base was filled with rumors. One word was current: "overseas." It filled the barracks, the mess hall, the flying field. Even in the air you heard it, passing from pilot to pilot four miles above the earth. It was a synonym for separation, that I knew. Then other words were added: Hickam Field, Wake Island, the Philippines. That was what was meant by overseas. It meant battle; it meant many would fall. All around me passed hints of the future: aircraft being battle-painted, troops moving, defenses being strengthened, girls continuously arriving and marching from the train to the wedding chapel. And of course there were tears.

In this confusion, this daily change, last month was unrecountable; last year meant only a formal measurement of time. True, I had realized that war was possible, even probable; it was not the war as such that affected me. Rather was it that I had become suddenly unbalanced by it, that I had lost sight of all permanency. That was what bothered me. In this transitory time, I had nothing to hold to, not even a secured buoy which could landmark my course when I left, or if I returned.

I thought of my family, but they were an entity in themselves. I wanted more than that. I wanted Janet. I did not ask myself or anyone else if it was fair. I asked only her.

San Diego in 1942 was not the place I would have wanted my bride to come to, but there was no opportunity for choice. She came not to a bridal bower, but to an arsenal. That was San Diego. All day and all night the sky bumbled with wheeling echelons of aircraft, while on the earth the factories breathed out black clouds of smoke that settle on man and stone alike. It was overdeveloped and overcrowded, a war city, a boom town.

We found our "little white cottage" on Alameda Street, in Coronado, a section near the air base and crowded with service families. It was furnished in a bare essential sort of way, a hybrid, attached dwelling, a cross that suggested neither home nor hotel. There Janet came, and to this new environment she accustomed herself quickly. There was no other

27

tempo for us. In desperate haste, we tried to live through honeymoon and happy-ever-after in whatever time was allowed us by the hasty orders and necessities of the Navy Department.

We even had a little dog, Twink, a wire-haired terrier that begged for a home from a store window in Chula Vista. For all the nuisance he was, he added much to our laughter and happiness. Every evening when I returned from the base, I would feed him his dose of cod liver oil from a huge spoon. Often this would be Janet's cue to make mock complaints of alienation of affection, lack of understanding, incompatibility, and the many other ills that some couples, who think of time as something on the clock, can create or invent.

We had friends, many of them. Wherever there is a community of service people, you will find no other way. There were cliques. We belonged to one. The glue that held us together was our job, our future, one way or the other. There were Bill Norval and his wife from Peoria, Illinois. As every soldier boasts of a buddy, he was mine. A big broad-shouldered fellow, he contrasted sharply with his pretty, small wife. And there were Joe Shoemaker and his wife, Mary. Again a contrast. He was short and solidly built; she was tall. There were Rad Arner, my instructor, and his wife, Edna, and brand new son, Skip. Then there were John Massey of Georgia, Tommy Gratzek of St. Paul, Maurice Ward of Kansas City, Paul Hagedorn of Jersey, and many others. They were all good friends. What more can be said?

When we went out, we went generally in a crowd, all of us piling into someone's car, laughing, sometimes too loudly. On some evenings Janet and I went alone.

We'd go to a movie, to a restaurant, to any place she wanted. I think she got a kick out of holding on to my arm when I returned a salute on the street. I'm glad she is proud of me; that would make anything worth while.

During the day, when I was at the base, Janet and the other girls could usually be found sitting on our small patch of lawn, knitting, identifying the planes in the sky, and probably swapping a little gossip on the side.

The routine at the base was routine; there is no other way to describe it. I generally reached there for an eight o'clock muster. If an early flight was scheduled, the hour was advanced to six o'clock. We flew long, arduous hours practicing maneuvers. Now and then the steadiness of the program was broken—when we flew out to sea in search of missing men. But February had arrived and was passing, and still no orders came. Though we realized the necessity for the absence of notice in advance of embarkation, this realization was ineffectual as a tonic for our restlessness. We wanted to know: *when?*

Often I broke the monotony of flight procedure by flying very low over the house and blimping the motor as my signal to Janet. If I saw her on the lawn, and the wind was right, I flew even lower, waving my hand and dipping my wings to her. How I would have loved to do that in Brooklyn!

In this same vein, I remember another time when our entire flight went tail-chasing and hedge-hopping, the favorite aerial game and practice of all military pilots. The target chosen was a power line on Catalina Island. In follow-the-leader fashion, the run began. One after the other, each plane streaked only a few feet off the ground toward the target, reached it, zoomed over it. Roger Crow, Bill Norval, Bill Foley, and then it was George Bastian's turn. He came in fast, very fast, he was getting close, closer, too close! His nose came up briefly as he tried to pull up; then it swerved crazily as it hit the wire. For a freezing second it appeared as though a bad crash was certain, but somehow George recovered control, and his ship climbed, with thirty feet of Catalina Island's main power line whipping from its wing! That day all of us had to sign a pledge, swearing that we would do no more hedge-hopping. And that night Catalina Island succumbed to an unscheduled, unrehearsed, and involuntary blackout.

The days were passing swiftly. There seemed to be a new tension about the base. It seemed as though orders were more imminent than ever—if that were possible.

My orders finally came on March 25, a Wednesday. Our flight had been relieved for the day, and I had arrived home early. It was a little past noon; Rad Arner and I were fighting the heat with tall glasses of beer, while Janet sat in her favorite chair knitting and talking and looking very content.

I was just about to refill Rad's glass when the telephone rang. Janet looked up at Rad and smiled. She said, "This is one time I don't have to worry, Rad. Since you're the flight boss and you're here with us, it can't mean orders."

Her words were in my ears as I lifted the receiver. It was Paul Hagedorn calling from the base. As I listened to his words, I saw that look of contentment fade from Janet's face. When I put down the phone I didn't have to tell her the news. It was as though through some sense she had felt every word I had listened to. I wished with all my might she wouldn't cry. I felt helpless enough as it was in leaving her. She didn't cry. That must have made it hurt her twice as much.

I had but four hours to do a thousand necessary things; at four o'clock I was due on the train. Rad and Edna pitched in to get the situation in hand, Janet had to stencil all the new gear I had recently acquired, friends who had heard the news called, Twink ran all about the house, barking, climbing into opened luggage, demanding attention. Bedlam is the only word to describe it all.

As soon as I could break away, I drove down to the base to pick up my orders. The sergeant handed them to me, an impersonal, mimeographed sheet. "By order of the Navy Department..." it ran, and after all the official terminology came our names, listed according to rank and the alphabet. I found mine: *"2nd Lieut. Moore, Thomas F., U.S.M.C.R."* That was all.

When I returned home the important things were done. We piled the bags into my Ford and took off for the station. Among Rad, Edna, and the heavy traffic, I could find little to say to Janet, and there was so much to say. About the only speech I could manage was in swearing at the cars that were delaying us, swearing at my watch, and kissing Janet whenever I had the chance.

We arrived at the station a moment too late, and for the next few minutes I had awful visions of my fate before a court-martial. But this concern was soon relieved with the appearance of eighteen other late comers, assembled by Mrs. Lofton Henderson, Major Henderson's wife. At her suggestion, we telephoned the Colonel. After a few sharp reminders about punctuality, he instructed us to take the next train which was to leave at eight o'clock in the evening. Many of the girls had not found time to cry. They had time now, four hours' worth. Until the next train north.

As if by magic, several bottles appeared, and the bachelors of the company amused themselves by making their contents disappear. There was nothing else to do.

Our group kept close together as the hours passed. Somebody told us that Major Henderson had dropped three of his four bags, one after the other, racing after the train. The story caused a brittle laugh. But the story came back to me at Midway, when Major Henderson went after that Jap carrier. It was with the same purposeful abandon as he went after the train.

The station was jammed with troops on the move, and for almost every soldier, sailor, and marine, there were wives, mothers, sweethearts, to cry for them, to kiss them, to hold them briefly. It was exactly as they picture it in the films, those lingering farewells; but no one was there to shout, "Cut!" or any other word that would bring this scene to an end. When the conductor said the words "All aboard!" it would mean *all aboard!* There was no changing *this* script.

Bill Norval came down from the base to see me off. He brought me a Hershey bar and a penny-for-luck. Those were his farewell presents, and the words, "Take care of yourself, Tom. You're on your own now." We shook hands for the last time at the station. My friend was killed a week later in an operational training flight.

Even now I could find little to say to Janet, although I looked at her often. I wanted to remember her face, remember it well. Then as the lights in the station went up, it grew close to eight o'clock—traintime.

We moved out onto the station platform, all of us.

32

It was nerve-racking watching the trainmen glancing at their oversized timepieces, the porters helping passengers into the cars. Already many were seated. Around us were wives, all newly wedded, clinging to their husbands, tear-staining uniforms. Only Janet was silent, very silent. She had tried her best, in the very brief time allowed us, to be bride and wife to me. I felt so very grateful to her, but I could say so very little. We had no more hours now—only a very few minutes. Time was mercilessly on schedule. We kissed. I said, "Good-by, Janet." I boarded the train.

From my compartment window I watched Janet and my friends and waved to them. Then a whistle blew and the train lurched forward suddenly, lurched again and again. We were moving. We waved now, not to our friends but to the lonely figure who was our own.

The little group was moving farther and farther from us. Then one girl, a bride of less than two weeks, detached herself from the others and ran sobbing down the platform after our train, crying a name that only her husband must have understood. He stood beside me watching her dash hopelessly toward him. It was his last picture of her. He failed to return from an attack at Midway.

I kept watching Janet, little Janet, getting littler and littler. My collar was choking me hard. A fear shot through me that if I did not return maybe she could belong to someone else. Then she blurred.

It must have been the light.

5. *Outward Bound*

Our train halted at Los Angeles, and there, at the Biltmore Hotel, we caught up with the other group and spent the night.

It was there, also, that I first met Major Lofton Henderson, and by the time we entrained for our embarkation port next morning I had decided that here was a man worthy of emulation. He was that kind of person, the kind you become aware of from the first handclasp. My knowing him, however, did not have long to flourish; that I deeply regret. This journey which we were beginning was the beginning of the end for him. It was the beginning of many ends.

This is how it started for all of us:

Several days after our arrival at the port we were awakened early one morning and told to ready ourselves for departure; a transport was preparing to leave for Hawaii. An hour later we were all assembled in the lobby of the Mark Hopkins Hotel, and from there a small caravan of taxicabs carried us across the city to the waterfront, to the address the orders had named *"Place of embarkation."*

The pier was clogged with troops. No, not troops. No American can be described as a troop—not at a *place of embarkation*. They were just a great number of somebody's sons, husbands, and brothers. They were just the boys with their big blue barracks bags waiting patiently to go on board the ship so they could go to where the war was.

34

Somehow the scene reminded me of Christmas. I don't know why. Maybe it was because it made Christmas seem so far away. There was no singing. Now and then some command would crack out and you heard it above the dull kind of noise that arises when a thousand men speak quietly.

For almost an hour we waited for orders to board ship, but no one was boarding. Major Henderson went off to investigate the delay, and when he returned he informed us that it was very possible we would not sail at all. A strike had developed among the ship's crew. They wanted a bonus for the trip through the war-zoned waters.

At this news many of the men went off to telephone their wives, but I remained. I did not want to surprise Janet with "possibilities"—and follow the news with a disappointment.

I noticed the ship. Lord, she was big! She was one of the biggest I had ever seen. In fact, she looked even familiar. Under heavy layers of a gray-brown paint she should have looked grim and warlike; but beneath it all I could still see something stately about her, something that suggested music and tuxedos, alligator luggage and shuffleboard. And I was right! Here, moored to this dock, passing smoke from her funnels in camouflaged anonymity, was a symbolic offering from our ally, Britain. The ship was a crack Cunard Liner.

The strike was settled at about two o'clock in the afternoon, and the soldiers began to march aboard. Major Henderson assembled us, issued our cabin numbers, and we too were ordered to embark.

As I stepped on the gangway and walked across it toward the ship, noticing the narrow canal of dirty water between the vessel and the shore, I thought many thoughts with every footstep. I can't remember even one today; there were too many.

Separated from the others by crowds of moving soldiers, I at last located my stateroom on C Deck. As I opened the door, the voices behind it united in a groan.

"What the hell, another one?"

"Welcome to the Black Hole of Calcutta!"

"I'll never eat a canned sardine again—I'll feel too sorry for him."

That cabin was crowded! In a space originally designed for two, nine of us had been billeted. All former luxuries of the room had been removed. The portholes had been covered with black paint, and electric bulbs alone provided the light. Against the walls beds were racked in tiers of three. It appeared that problems would arise for choosing the favored positions. However, when they did, a few minutes later, a pair of dice bounced across the floor and all questions were decided quickly.

Several hours later, a lower berth and fifty dollars to the good, I went up on deck. The soldiers had all come aboard, and, except for a few military policemen still walking about, the pier was like a huge ball park after the game is over. It looked lonesome and very empty. You could see the street, looking as it always looked in late afternoon, a street on which taxicabs raced, a policeman blew his whistle, and people walked. It reminded me of West Street, in New York.

I watched as they took down the gangways and set free the shore lines with their cone-shaped rat guards. I remembered the legend which said that if the rats left the ship before the voyage began, the ship would not come home. But none ran back to the shore. It was a good sign.

I made my way aft through thick bunches of soldiers standing about on the deck. We would get under way soon now, very soon.

The motors began to throb. A huge foamy circle appeared at the stern as the great propellers began turning. They turned faster, and the foam circle grew wider, longer. The propellers and the insistent little tugs were pushing us away from the land, away from home.

We stood watching, the soldiers and I, watching the land as we left it. It was then—just then as we left the land—that the words "my country" became real with meaning. I tried to photograph every acre of it in my memory. I tried to remember every piece of it I had seen, and every piece I hadn't seen I tried to imagine. Above all, I wanted to come back to it!

In the group of soldiers around me, one spoke up: "I wish we were going out from New York."

"How's that?" another asked. "You from New York?"

"Naw, I'm from Indianapolis. But the Statue of Liberty is in New York, and I ain't ever seen it. I think it woulda been nice seeing it now."

A pause. "Yeah," agreed the other.

"Yeah," said the soldier from Indianapolis.

Yeah.

On the next morning I awoke to find that we had been joined by another troop transport and a convoying destroyer that cruised around and around the two ships like a watchful shepherd.

After a very plentiful English breakfast, we returned to our cabin, and The Great Crap Game began.

37

It lasted till our voyage ended. There was nothing else to do. No radios were permitted; the sea was tiring to look at; fellow passengers were all of one general occupation, and every group was set apart from each other by a strict code of rank.

Like all transports, she was a dry ship. The cocktail lounge had been converted to accommodate card-playing, considered by recognition the most dignified type of gaming. Undignified dice-throwing was confined to space behind locked stateroom doors. Our group, not being of a too dignified nature, favored this speakeasy recreation as our choice for whiling away the miles and the hours.

So these were the sounds that drifted through the seldom opened door of our cabin from morning to night to morning again:

"...Dice, dice be good to me!"..."Roll out, you bones. Roll out and bring home a barrel of gold!"... "My point is eight—come eight!"... "Eights skate and duplicate!"... "Seven! Seven, you're dead!"... "Who'll fade twenty?"—"Shoot! Shoot, you're faded!"... "Right!"... "Six!"... "Nine! Nina from Pasadena... Five bucks no ten-eleven!"... "Crap!"... "Four!"... "Five!"... "Eight!"

Sold American!

The smoke that hung in the air inside the room was thicker than I could stand, and I decided to go up on deck for a stroll. When I began to search through my bags for a leather flying jacket to put on, the mess we had made in hurried packing became very much in evidence. I discovered my toothpaste in a night slipper, a pair of socks in the pocket of a shirt. I was lifting these and other things out to repack, when all at once a raucous burst of laughter rocked the room as I found

38

myself lifting one of Janet's dresses high in the air! How it got there, I'll never know. Perhaps Twink had dragged it in as his contribution toward hastening my departure. But it stopped the crap game for a few minutes, and even Bill Rogers, our sleeping beauty, awoke, looked, and laughed before he tumbled back to slumber.

When the laughter was over and the dice began to skip across the floor again, I packed away the dress, slipped on my leather jacket, and went up on deck. Though I had tried to forget her—I had to forget her now!—the sight and feel of that dress brought her back to me, vividly and disturbingly. She was in my mind now as I walked around and around from bow to stern, and from stern to bow again . . . she and the child that would be hers and mine. . . .

A few days out, while the Army band on deck was pounding its cymbals, beating its drums, and blowing its mammoth tubas in a blaring rendition of "The Caissons Go Rolling Along," short, happy-go-lucky Lieutenant Jack Foeller of the U. S. Marines discovered his tiny ocarina. Rolling dice with one hand, he went into competition with the Army, playing without end the "Marine Hymn." To the other players, the combination was deafening and terrible, and, to a man, everyone in the room made for Foeller, who, still playing his ocarina, kept leaping out of reach with the agility of a monkey. Then, just as John Massey grabbed him, the *Abandon Ship* alarm sounded through the corridors.

"Abandon ship! Abandon ship!" cried Foeller. "Let go of me. Don't you hear it?"

"Abandon ship hell!" roared Massey. "The only thing that abandons this ship is that goddam midget juke-box of yours!"

Someone opened the porthole and two seconds later the ocarina went sailing through it. That done, we hurried to our stations for the lifeboat drill. I don't think Foeller saw his ocarina go. He spent many hours looking for it.

We had a steward, an underweight little Englishman with big teeth, whom we kept in a state of constant bewilderment with our behavior. It did not seem "quite the thing," as he put it, for officers to carry on without affected formality while he was present. But I think he liked us for that, because he treated us especially well. I liked to talk with him, and he with me. We entertained each other by our varied accents.

He told me he had not seen England for several years, and then he went on to say, "Yes, guv'nor. This is me last voyage. When I get back to England—bless 'er—I'm going to get me a farm and live off of the land. I'm finished with the sea. This is me last voyage." He was a typical seaman. Those old words identified him anywhere.

It was growing warmer now as we sailed toward southern latitudes. The submarine menace was growing as we proceeded, and, accordingly, lifeboat drills were held more frequently. Often our escorting destroyer would race off under full steam, circle an area, and return. It was a good show, an intermediary act between the crap game.

The next day was Easter Sunday. Catholic services were held in one of the spacious lounges, into which a portable altar had been wheeled. It was the most unusual Easter Sunday Mass I had ever attended.

Father Egan, an Army chaplain, stood before the altar conducting the service. A life belt lay beside him, its bright yellow color in sharp contrast to his raiments. It was a reminder that though we prayed and kneeled and uttered words before God, we were also close to the enemy.

That night the dice game reached its highest pitch. In the morning we would arrive at Pearl Harbor, and after that—we knew not what. I tried to imagine what would come with days in the near future. I even tried to exaggerate my imagination, but even so, my fancies ended far short of reality. The others, too, were affected. I could tell by the slow pace with which the dice began to fall. There was a lessening of talk and laughter, and we put the dice away early.

Land was sighted at dawn.

6. *Via Pearl Harbor*

There were no flowers afloat in the bay as our ship sought anchorage. Vainly, we thousands lined the deck railings searching out the advertised sights of Hawaii—the grass skirts, the singing guitars, the garlanded swimmers diving for silver. But the banks and the bay were silent, vigilantly silent. Then, after a long watch, it became obvious to us on this April morning that the Islands had long ago stored away their toys and tinsel; even the word *"Aloha!"* We had come not as dolls to people a dolls' house, but as soldiers to garrison a fortress.

Diamond Head, the Royal Hawaiian, the Hotel Moana—we made out these landmarks and approved them. Our group, bunched closely together, were exchanging comments upon these places when, from up forward, a hoarse voice cried out the electric command: "Look!"—and we all looked.

In water twelve fathoms deep lay a ship, all broken and half sunk. The bow stuck up through the water like the pointing finger of a man frozen dead. For less than a second there was a sudden silence, followed by a burst of *Gees* and *wows, holy smokes* and *the dirty rats.* But even in these exclamations a note of shock was very evident—shock at actually *seeing* an American ship torn and defeated. An American ship, which American minds had conceived and American hands had built. American hearts had sailed it. Now American men lay dead within it. American—like us.

42

I suppose I should have thought some spirited thoughts then: thoughts of vengeance, anger—anything dramatic, anything spirited. But my mind was too numbed for such thinking, too numbed to be suddenly brave or suddenly afraid. And as we sailed past that quiet place I could bring myself to do nothing but watch, in quiet review.

We tied up alongside a pier near Honolulu, and in a little while we disembarked. Here again there were neither cheers nor brassy music at our arrival, nor *leis* cast upon our shoulders. There was just a mild-faced transport officer from Ewa Field, detailed to meet us and escort us back to the base.

Our baggage was loaded on a Marine van, while we were led to an olive-drab bus. As soon as the major and captains were seated, the rest of us, like respectable tourists, scrambled for the window positions that remained, and soon our bus was under way, riding over the macadam highway fronting the sea. For perhaps fifteen minutes there was nothing in the shape of a view. Palm trees, bushes, and Coca-Cola signs screened the water. Then the road curved and climbed above these barriers.

"Hey! Will you look at that." The voice came from a front seat.

We looked, and again there were half-sunken ships to see.

"There's the *Arizona!* Damn those—"

"And the *Utah!*"

A long, low whistle. "Boy-oh-boy-oh-boy."

The road curved again, and again the sea was screened. For a while no one spoke, then:

"We'll show 'em. Boy-oh-boy, we'll show 'em."

43

Ewa Air Base was a long stretch of flat ground criss-crossed by concrete runways and flanked by hangars, barracks, and administration shacks. It was a reception center, and from the very first I knew that my stay here would not be permanent. I was assigned to no particular squadron and was treated with the casual attitude suggestive of one who has arrived only to rest and go on.

On December 7 the base had been attacked. It had not been damaged severely, not as compared to Hickam, but it had been damaged enough for those who had been there to avoid mentioning it. When I asked, I was answered in abrupt phrases or sentences, seldom in paragraphs. Everyone seemed to have been left with a different impression predominant. These are a few that I heard:

"The bastards came down like bats out of hell laying hundred pounders all over the field...."

"The Japs? —— 'em!"

"... It took three days to bury those sailors—you hear me? Three days!"

"... I was having a powwow with the sandman when they arrived, so I hit the deck, grabbed a gun, and went racing outside in the top half of my pajamas. Well, I began firing at them, and dammit I kept worrying that if I did get knocked off, I didn't want to be found in that kind of uniform...."

"... Most of our planes never got off the ground. They were knocked for a splintered crap house in the first run...."

"Those planes we saw looked good and plenty fast, but when one of our boys got a bead on one, he just broke apart like a clay pipe after a few rounds."

"...But they got us good all right, and don't think those babies can't fly."

"...What the hell, who wants to live forever?"

I had few duties but to wait. Sometimes I imagined the war would end, and I would be left still waiting, but when I remembered that the war was only four months old and that I was a thousand miles closer to it now than last week, I knew it would not end before I played my scene.

Once I flew, just once. I ferried a plane from Ford Island to Ewa, and I saw Hawaii as the Japs had seen it. Somehow it was difficult to conceive that the enemy had flown through these very spaces in which I was flying, that the quiet earth below had been ripped by bombs and erupted skyward, that those irregularly spaced patches in the green below were scars from that bombing. It just seemed unbelievable.

I didn't like Hawaii, not in the least. I had imagined it as it had been pictured, an actual garden of Eden in technicolor, where nothing was planned, but everything impulsively created. Yeah! It was more like a nurtured botanical garden, a hothouse created especially for the eighteen-day tour at $299.99 and up per person, guide and hotel included. Now the war had come to it in hobnailed boots, trespassing on the make-believe scenery and throwing rocks at the hothouses.

I continued to wait and it was hell. I wanted to become part of an operating unit, with my duties clear and defined. The uncertainty of San Diego was just as prevalent here. To my prejudiced eye, it seemed as though everything was in turmoil and confusion through which I must wait, wait, wait.

There was one comforting thought, however: Major

Henderson was also still unassigned, and I wanted to serve with him and under him. So if I held my breath whenever an operations orderly came near me it was mainly because I wanted so much to travel away in the company of friends.

At the end of almost a week, the waiting ended. I was handed a mimeographed notice—an emancipation proclamation!

> To:—Major Lofton R. Henderson, USMC
> 2nd Lieuts. Thomas J. Gratzek, USMCR
> Bruno P. Hagedorn, USMCR
> Thomas F. Moore, Jr., USMCR
> Jesse D. Rollow, Jr., USMCR
> Harold G. Schlendering, USMCR
> Maurice Ward, USMCR
> Subject: Change of station.
> You will stand detached from Headquarters and Service Squadron 21, Marine Aircraft Group 21, on April 11, 1942 . . . and will proceed and embark as directed by oral instructions to Marine Aircraft Group 22, wherever that group may be, and upon arrival report to the commanding officer thereof, for assignment to aviation duty with that group. . . .

"That group" was stationed at Midway.

On a morning several days later, we were taken back to the same place where we had previously landed. There, moored to the dock lay a small Naval transport loading for sailing.

We were not the only passengers to board. We had as company a contingent of about 150 Marine ground troops, who had also been transferred to the island. I remember standing near the deck railing to watch their faces as they trooped aboard. They were young faces, marked with the characteristics of many nations.

46

One I remember in particular. He was a little fellow, and his face seemed absurdly childlike under his round steel helmet. It was the kind of face that would appear more in place beneath the brim of a Boy Scout hat. His heavy bag and heavy rifle were giving him some trouble. They were so big, and he was so small. He was grunting and sweating under the bulky weight, as he stepped upon the narrow gangway. But then, as he saw me smiling down at him, he glared back at the challenge and suddenly became filled with the strength of a hundred men. Balancing his load with one gesture, he squared his thin shoulders and went marching up the plank to salute the colors with a resolution that suggested Sherman marching to the sea.

Somehow, in that moment, I felt I had seen a part of that something vaguely called "American spirit." And that is why I remember and mention the incident.

There was no delay in our leaving. We waited for neither time nor tide, only for the order. Shortly thereafter the order was given, and we set sail for Midway Island—twelve hundred miles to the northwest of Hawaii, and twelve hundred miles closer to the enemy.

This voyage was different from the last. The thought of Midway sobered us all. It was to be expected that we would see action there. Had not the Japs attacked and taken every one of the other links in the American chain from Pearl Harbor to Hong Kong? Only Midway remained—Midway, the climactic prize. From Midway the Japanese could send their long-range bombers to attack Hawaii steadily. It took hardly any reasoning at all to guess that they would make a bid for it, and a heavy bid at that.

On one of the nights we were at sea, I took my station to stand my four-hour watch. They were lonely

47

hours. The wind was still, the sea was calm, and in the sky the millions and millions of stars were each sharp and clear and glittering. Stars over the Pacific. How quickly they could run! Six hours before, this same sky had been over Times Square, over home. Home . . . all through my watch I thought of what that word had come to mean.

There was little to do aboard ship. It was too small to allow for anything but necessities. It's only compromise with luxury was a small library in the wardroom. Here I spent much of my time. On one of our first days at sea, I chanced to open a copy of William L. Shirer's *Berlin Diary*. It was a new experience. I read that book well; I read it though it disturbed me, and smashed my rose-colored glasses, and shouted things so loudly I could not help but listen. It explained a lot of things. When I had finished it, the cry, "Midway Island off the starb'd bow," had already been uttered, and in some small way, I felt as though I knew a little bit about why I had come here.

Midway Island! One and a half square miles of it.
One and a half square miles of sand and coral sur-
rounded by barbed wire and the sea; one and a half
square miles of bleak and open ground, flattened by
the sweeping winds, washed by driving rains, and
burning beneath a tyrant sun; one and a half square
miles populated only by men in uniform and a variety
of pelicans; one and a half square miles of guns, guns,
guns, ready and waiting to go off.

When we arrived at the air base, I found it to be
much larger than I had expected. It was fitted with concrete runways that stretched as long as a mile in
length. In the pits alongside the field stood our planes,
kept in constant readiness. I could see mechanics hover-
ing over them, seemingly nursing them. And even at
that moment a patrol was circling the field preparing
to land, while another flight was being readied for
take-off.

At headquarters, our entire group of seven was assigned en masse to Marine Dive Bomber Squadron 241,
to which Major Henderson was appointed as Commander. When these formalities were ended, Colonel
Wallace, commanding all Marine aviation on the island,
escorted us to the mess hall, a wooden, barrack-type
structure that served also as saloon, social club, and
church—depending upon the occasion and the weather.
There we were introduced to our squadron mates.

A meet-the-boys attitude prevailed. Those who had

49

been stationed here on the island but a few weeks had been graduated from flying school a few weeks ahead of me, and these I knew and recognized. But there were others, with captains' bars pinned to their collars, who were strangers. They replied to their names with a curt nod and a brief handshake, at the same time completely appraising us with one brief squint. Some of them had been stationed here for almost as long as six months, a period that was marked with the attack upon Pearl Harbor, the fall of the Philippines, Guam, and Wake Island. Now and again during that period, enemy warships had shelled the island, but these incidents had been minor. Thus, for those months they had done nothing but wait, wait for the full fury to strike Midway. Those months of waiting were written across their faces sharply and clearly; it did not make them look younger—but then, nothing that happened to us made us look younger.

In talking with these men I became aware that, beneath all the smiles and good humor, they were drawn tight as the strings of a finely tuned violin, and if one were to pluck these strings the result would be shattering and explosive. It was a conscious strain even to talk with them, always to say the right thing at the right time, to be firm in expressing an opinion, and yet inoffensive. I was unused to such rigid self-control, and when evening came and I went to the dugout to which most of our group had been assigned, Maurice Ward and I blew up at each other in an argument that almost ended in a fist fight.

It was just that the boys had all gone to the dugout ahead of me, and, quite naturally, the first to arrive had grabbed the choice sleeping locations—namely, the top bunks. So, when I stumbled down the narrow steps into our tiny underground hut and found that the top bunks were already occupied, I loudly disapproved of the arrangement. Because Major Henderson was there, I covered my temper with a lying smile, and made a stump speech for my rights.

Since Schlendering and Rollow said nothing, I turned on Ward and demanded that the four of us pick cards for the choice bunks. But Ward was adamant and ignoring. He continued to read his book though I shouted and ranted for fair play. When he did reply, it was with just a few quiet, biting words. Then we became more and more abusive of each other, but carefully so—Major Henderson was present. Jokingly, I made the statement that my commission was dated prior to his own, and so I outranked him; whereupon someone, attracted by the noise coming from our dugout, stuck his head inside and shouted, "Rank among second lieutenants is like virginity among whores! Shut up and go to sleep!"

We all laughed and the tension was broken. Ward said he just wanted to see how mad I'd get and then we agreed to pick cards. That almost started the battle all over again. I claimed that high card won in Brooklyn, while Ward said that low card won in Missouri. Major Henderson was smiling and finally handed down a decision. We picked cards and again I won. Then I told Ward that I didn't want a top bunk anyway, so we all went to sleep as happy as homesick men can be.

The next morning a truck carried us to our planes. Waiting beside my ship I found a tall slim young Marine captain. We introduced ourselves again; we had met in the mess hall the day before but had forgotten each other's names. He was Dick Fleming and he gave me the cockpit checkout on the SB2U.

The planes we flew were ancient fabric-covered SB2U's, and they had not improved with age. In fact, though they were designated as dive bombers, they could not be dived safely at too steep an angle. We were all more than just a little worried about the prospect of having to use them in a real attack. The word was that new SBD's would soon arrive, but the word was also worn with age.

In our spare hours we tried to keep ourselves occupied in the best possible manner. The important thing was amusement. And because we couldn't buy it, we improvised. We threw cards, played ping-pong, read books, and intoxicated the clumsy, bony gony birds. They were our favorite amusement.

I bought a piano accordion from Captain Elmer Glidden and tore the stillness from the night with howling sound. Captain Armand De Lalio had another one sent to him from Pearl Harbor, and together we made everything but music. There was, however, one musician in the squadron. Captain Dick Fleming, an accomplished pianist before the war, rescued from us the ravaged reputations of many composers when he handled my accordion. So, a glee club was often assembled when things were dull, and while Mars' minstrel played we sang ourselves to laughter.

. We were defending an American outpost, which we had come a long way from home to defend. It was the middle of May. Our country had been at war for five months. Many of our comrades in arms had made the supreme sacrifice, and we in our turn were awaiting the moment when we, too, would be called upon at least to offer that sacrifice. But I must here note and mention that, though all these things held a very definite truth, we were, to say the least, unaware in the ultimate sense of what that truth concerned.

There was a time when we were gathered in the mess hall deploying through bottles of beer and the question of "Why the war?" was broached. The variety of opinions voiced at that session differed with almost each man present. But in no single opinion could I find any reason that was as strong as even the little pieces of steel we were so soon to face.

"We're fighting because we were attacked. We've got to show them who's boss."

"Yeah? Well, the life of even one man is a hell of a price to pay for that kind of a show."

"Ah, it's a money war. We fight and they collect."

"Is that so?"—from a banker's son. "What the hell do you think I'm doing here?"

Of course, there were many who expressed no opinion. I like to think that they felt too deeply about it to say anything.

There was much mention, naturally, of the word "freedom" and much talk of "issues," but they were intangibles. We spoke of them in that way. As for myself, I did not think too much about it. I had not yet actually seen men die for any of those things.

Toward the end of May a ship arrived at Midway carrying our long-promised new planes as well as ten or fifteen additional flyers to complement both our own squadron and the fighter squadron which had shared the field. At about the same time a contingent of Army Flying Fortresses also landed to operate from our base. A squadron of Navy P boats followed and immediately began a daily patrol. The appearance of these important reinforcements gave rise to wide speculation about the imminence of an enemy attack—after all, you never sharpen a knife unless you plan to use it. We had been engaged in daily maneuvers before, but from that date forward they were so realistically planned and executed that all previous maneuvers seemed more like games, now that we looked back.

It was some nights later, as we were preparing to turn in, when someone—I believe it was Maurice Ward—asked Major Henderson about the imminence of such an attack. As always, Major Henderson was objective. He told us his opinion in these words:

"The success of all our Pacific operations depends upon us—and, gentlemen, I make no understatement when I use the word 'us.' We are the shock troops that must meet any attack that may come. There is no one between us and the enemy. Remember that. We must recognize that responsibility, each and every one of us. . . ."

I looked about our little underground room. So there was just us and others like us. . . .

And who composed *us?*

Major Lofton P. Henderson, age 39: Professional officer, graduate of the United States Naval Academy. All his interests in life had always been subjected to the military service. It was for such moments as these to which his life for more than twenty years had been dedicated.

Lieutenant Gilbert Schlendering, age 23: Quiet, a thinker, an intellectual. "I fight so that I can read what I want to read, and listen to what I want to listen to, and live as I wish to live."

Second Lieutenant Maurice Ward, age 22: A tall, lanky boy from Kansas City, Missouri. I always thought of him as someone who had stepped from the college classroom straight to Midway, stopping only long enough to leave his books and change his clothes.

Second Lieutenant Jesse Rollow, age 24: Always good for a laugh, firm in his opinions, cocky, but sensitive; a good civilian trying to be a good soldier.

Second Lieutenant Thomas F. Moore, Jr., age 24: The eternal plebeian New Yorker no matter what the conditions or where the place.

That was part of us.

On the night of June 3 I returned from my alert station carrying some beer and cheese sandwiches from the mess hall. Two of these sandwiches were almost sodden with mustard because that was the way Major Henderson liked them. When I entered the dugout I found only the Major there. I was glad he was alone. He was like Father Woloch, a man you could talk to with no fear of being misunderstood.

There had been many nights like this before, but somehow this night was different. There was something in the air, I just felt it; we all felt it. No one knew what it was exactly, but whatever it was it made us feel more than a little nervous and more than a little tense. That was why I was glad to talk alone with Major Henderson. Though he always knew that come what may he must lead us all, he was never disturbed, nor had I ever seen him break the evenness of his temper. Talking with him always made me feel more calm.

On this night, over beer and cheese sandwiches, we talked about the enemy, the Japanese enemy. He spoke his opinion evenly and without passion; as always he was objective.

"They are like a horde of impudent germs that are trying to disease the world. The more you kill the less grows the danger. They must be made to suffer because

55

only by suffering will they realize that the world is not afraid of them, and the only way to do that is to destroy enough of them so that those who live will realize that they must never play with fire again. Kill them, lots of them, and all their organs will burst like balloons. They have got to be killed as you kill a fly, without pity, without remorse."

One by one, the other boys strolled in: first Schlendering, then Ward, then Rollow. We all talked together for a while and when we ran out of words Schlendering and Ward climbed up into their bunks to continue the books they had been reading, Major Henderson turned to writing a report, and Rollow and I carried on with a discussion of the baseball scores we had heard at the engineering tent. We did not know then that several of our Naval patrol planes had just returned to Midway after making contact with the enemy, and that the enemy was a Japanese flotilla on its way to attack and invade us.

About ten o'clock the light was extinguished and we turned in. There were all five of us in the dugout that night. All the beds were filled: Major Henderson, Jesse Rollow, Gil Schlendering, Maurice Ward, and myself. We were five.

Five.

"C'mon, hit the deck! Hit the deck!"

The voice traveled miles through the fogs of sleep, and then, after a long time, I heard it and opened my eyes. Someone had switched on the light. I looked around. Major Henderson was out, and already Rollow, Ward, and Schlendering were dressing.

"What"—I yawned—"the hell! I'm sleepy."

Rollow, sitting in the bunk near mine, began to bang his shoe on a piece of iron pipe near my pillow. "Get up out of that flea bag!" he shouted above the din. "Get up! Get up! Get up!"

That noise was too much. I climbed out of my bunk and began to dress. Glancing at my watch, I found it to be only a few minutes past three A.M. Well, this must be it; this was not just another alert. The waiting was ended. Looking about the room, I could see that I was not alone in my opinion. Using a *Saturday Evening Post* across his knees as a desk, one of the boys was writing a letter. No one had written letters at three o'clock in the morning before. . . .

When I had finished dressing, I made my way through pitch-black darkness to the mess hall. There I found the others of the dive-bombing and fighter squadrons already collected. I cannot recall the names or faces; I had seen them too often before to take notice of them now. But it seemed as though everyone had something to say. We were like people who keep talking all through a minor operation in order to keep their

57

minds active on other things than what the doctor is doing. So while we chewed on thick slices of bread with marmalade and drank burning hot swallows of coffee, we talked and talked. Who listened, I'll never know.

It was still not yet dawn when we made our way in groups of threes and fours to where the planes were waiting in pits. Private Huber, my gunner, was already there checking his guns and ammunition and whatever else he had to do. I didn't know Huber very well, but in just a few hours I was to find out a great deal about him.

"Everything shipshape, Huber?"

"Everything shipshape, sir."

A 500-pound bomb was in place under the fuselage. It looked deadly even there. I climbed into my cockpit and started the engine to warm it up in case a quick take-off was necessary; then I tried the radio and inter-com telephones. Everything was in order. Danny Iverson, who was in the pit next to mine, waved, and I waved back. There was nothing to do now but wait.

Perhaps I should write a short note to Janet; it could be written by the light from the instrument panel. No, I decided against it. It was too late for that now. If I was to write I wanted it to be something meaningful and everlasting in case I didn't come back. I couldn't think of any such words now. I could think only of her, and of our unborn baby. What would the baby be like? A boy or a girl? A boy, of course, and he would be named after my dad. Thomas F. Moore, III; it sounded almost like a king's name. What would he look like? Would he cry a lot? Sure! He'd cry just to show his spirit. How big would his fingers be? And his toes? *My* baby, *my* son. That was the hardest of all to imagine. . . . *God, let me live long enough to see him!*

In the east, the sun was beginning to bayonet away the night. Morning was coming. . . . An hour later it had arrived.

Major Henderson's plane started to taxi slowly along the runway that adjoined my position. As he approached, it appeared as though he were getting ready to take off on a routine patrol flight. Captain Zach Tyler ran out toward the moving plane, and when the Major saw him he stopped. Tyler bounced up on the wing and spoke a few words, then I saw Major Henderson's hand describe a slow, beckoning motion. Tyler ran back to his own plane and started getting ready. Then Danny Iverson began to move out on the runway. That was all I needed. Already the Major's plane was in the air.

"Okay, Huber, let's go!"

I gunned the engine and we moved out onto the runway. We headed into the wind, and then my hand pushed the throttle forward. We began to move faster and faster. The plane was straining to lift itself into the air when the engine started coughing and spitting. I knew I wasn't going to make it. I cut the throttle back sharply, intending to taxi the plane to the engineering shack and have the engine checked. Then I saw many more of my squadron mates taking off. I wanted to be with them. I decided to try it again. With some difficulty, we got into the air.

I had heard no formal command given, but our squadron was up. For almost a minute and a half there was nothing but the steady drone of our engine, and a few idle remarks passing over the phones. I was wondering whether we would see any enemy when suddenly over the radio came the unbelievable words:

59

"Attention! Attention! Island is now under heavy attack! Island is now under heavy attack! . . ."

I glanced backward. It was true—bombs were bursting all over the island. All at once a sheet of flame streaked toward heaven and fell back. Thick palls of smoke were climbing upward from three different places. We rendezvoused at a predetermined point. We fell into a box formation as we flew. Above, the sky was very blue and clean of clouds. The wind from the propeller whipped around my goggled eyes and face, but otherwise the weather was mild. Then Dick Fleming's voice came on directing a change in our course.

Major Henderson was some distance off to our right, flying a roving patrol scouting the enemy. He felt he was more apt to spot them if he didn't have to concentrate on his place in the formation.

The enemy! What would they be like? How would it be to attack them? To kill them?

My watch—it was a high school graduation gift from Mother and Dad—was marking off minute after minute, sixty of them . . . sixty-one . . . sixty-two . . . still we flew on.

I wished I had written that letter to Janet. She knew I was at Midway. Already the news of the battle's beginning must be on its way back home. . . . How would Janet react? How would Mother and Dad react? How would America react? It would depend on the outcome. . . . I was scared, no doubt about it. . . . What was Huber thinking?

"Everything okay, Huber?"

"Okay, sir."

I ordered him to recheck his guns and make sure they were in good working order. We'd be in this together, he and I. Rank had kept us apart; I hardly knew him.

But if we died today, we'd remain beneath the sea through eternity no more than five feet apart. It was a rub....

My watch showed eighty-three minutes from time of take-off ... eighty-four ... eighty-five ...

"Attention! Attention! All pilots, attention." It was Major Henderson's voice. "Two enemy carriers on our port bow! Enemy carriers on our port bow!..."

9. *This Was the Enemy*

"...Enemy carriers at ten o'clock. Attack enemy carriers!"

There they were! There were two and they were big. They left wakes that were two thin white lines upon the sea.... These two big bastards—this was the enemy!

The sound of our engines, the booming within me—it was like a big bass drum beating like hell under my shirt.

"...Enemy aircraft!...Enemy aircraft!—"

Suddenly, off to the left appeared a score of trim little airplanes, buzzing mosquito-like toward our formation. On their short stubby wings was marked an oversized red ball. Japs—Zero fighters—was all that registered as I saw them roll and twist against the sky and the sun. At first they looked almost playful; then they came down upon us. Quickly they grew from mosquitoes to sparrows, from sparrows to hawks, and, as their distance from us closed to no distance at all, they became warplanes firing a hundred lines of gray-white tracers that webbed in the air.

Now, above the sound of engines, I could hear the brittle rattle of machine guns. I saw them swoop down on friends flying near me. I saw my friends respond to the attack valiantly, hopelessly. They fired fast at the faster moving Zeros. Burst after burst of gunfire raced from friend to Zero, from Zero to friend. A Jap Zero veered and turned a hundred feet from me, pilot and motor dead. I heard the thin whine of the wind as it passed over his wings. A helmeted head lolled from side to side as the plane wobbled out of control. Then like a struck match he burst into flame and fell burning into the sea.

Still they came on. Two of them roared up behind us. Little holes were racing across our right wing. Bullets whipped into the instrument panel before me, shattering glass in all directions, shattering the radio equipment. My first and only reaction to this was, "God, here comes part of the Sixth Avenue El!" Huber opened fire. I heard the sharp bark of our gun throwing bullet after bullet at the Japs. It was a good sound, a comforting sound. Already one of them had turned away. The other was still behind us. Huber would get him. . . . All at once our gun stopped firing.

"My gun is jammed!" Huber yelled through the phones.

I was in no mood for this news. "For God's sake," I shouted back, "if you can't shoot the damn gun at least aim it at him! Make him think it's good! Scare him with it!"

I am not proud of that command, but there was nothing else to do. A bullet rang off the steel armored plate behind me. To hell with that sonofabitch! The sound of gunfire was now part of me. Its impression had been made and noted. I saw a friend ride into a blast of bullets that went in one side and passed out the other. I saw that friend begin to fall. A long trail of oily black smoke was bursting from beneath his engine like a ribbon unwinding from the tumbling plane.

Already many of the squadron had gone down upon the carriers. I was awaiting my turn. Though they could knock some of us to hell, they couldn't break our

63

formation. We would dive only when ready or only when dead.

Again and again and again the bastards came down, zooming under us, over us. Sometimes they passed Huber and me with only six or eight feet clearance, their machine guns giggling. Several bullets tore in and out of the fuselage—

Then I saw Blaine go into his dive. Now it was my turn! I kicked left—left rudder, left aileron—stick forward. We began to dive. Damn it all to hell, here we come!

Everything I had ever been taught about flying or bombing was cut so deep in me I never needed to think or remember. This was it! This was a live run! A real, live run! The bomb was armed; I checked it again and again. We were diving fast—as fast as three tons of dead weight tied to a thousand racing horses could dive. It was a sleigh ride, a damn bellywopping sleigh ride.

Down, down, down from eight thousand feet to the enemy. Below, a thick cloud bank was racing upward to meet us. In a second we were inside it, feeling its dampness, it coolness. Then, another second, and we were free of it.

There was the water. And up and down inside my sights was a carrier, a rectangular piece of enemy! We were dead upon it. No need to change direction; the cross-hairs divided it evenly. I checked my bomb again. It was growing bigger and bigger, filling the sights, filling them and now overlapping them. The wind was whining and shrieking in an unending high G.

Pull out! Pull out! A voice was shouting through to me. *Drop the bomb and pull out!*

I snapped back, glanced at the dials on the instrument panel. The needles were spinning crazily. The altimeter read five hundred feet and we still were diving straight on the target!

At four hundred feet I punched the bomb release and pulled the stick toward my stomach. The bomb fell clear. I never heard the explosion, but a wave of concussion smashed back at us, and we were thrown completely out of control.

For about five endless seconds I fought the drafts that gripped and tossed us down toward the sea. We dropped, climbed, and dropped again as the propeller spun and screamed. We were losing altitude— The water was less than forty short feet below—

Then, abruptly, we were free and clear again. Only twenty-five feet above the water, the airplane recovered its balance and motion. We began to skim the waves, gaining speed to regain altitude.

I looked back to see what damage our bomb had done to the carrier, and the view was suddenly blocked by the sight of three Jap fighters bearing down upon Huber and me—hell bent for destruction!

Futilely I pushed the throttle to its last advance notch, and the speed indicator needle began to climb to higher numbers; but the highest number on the dial was not high enough, not with the altimeter registering dangerously close to zero.

The Japs came on. Somewhere off in the sky ahead was a cloud bank, a refuge if I could reach it. But we would never make it in time; I knew we were going to get it and get it good. Still, it was a life ring, and I made my grab for it.

I heard the bastards warm their guns with a few short bursts of fire; they were estimating the range. I knew Huber was still positioning his gun. He was in a bad spot. He was helpless. Their guns began to rattle a jumbled tac-tac-tac—tac-tac-tac-tac-tac. . . . Their many guns against—what? Against a nineteen-year-old kid behind a useless weapon. Tracers streaked by us on all sides. "—— 'em! —— 'em!" I heard myself cry out a dozen times. The sound of their machine guns sounded above everything else, a sharp, angry noise. One of them was firing a long, long burst.

"I'M HIT!" Huber screamed. "I can't aim the gun any more . . ."

Hang on! Hang on! The cloud was closer now. I looked back at Huber. God! His face and chest were covered with splashes of blood. I thought he would soon die, and only two hours before—

Another burst, and another, and another. The bullets were close and deadly. They rang alarms as they struck all parts of the ship. The motor began to cough. It coughed four or five times and stopped. The propeller was turning in slower and slower circles. We started to nose down; I had to prepare for a water landing. The fuel line must be shot away. I switched tanks and grabbed for the wobble pump. I almost broke my hand reaching. From his rear seat Huber, wounded as he was, was already working it. The gasoline from the auxiliary tank was pressured to the engine. The motor coughed and caught; the propeller was spinning again. We were still flying!

Behind us the Japs had seen the engine quit, had seen us nose down toward the water. Two of them, thinking we were done, had pulled away. Now only one remained—that bastard!

He brought his plane into position above and before me; about two hundred yards separated us. I still pointed toward the cloud bank. Then that Jap turned

66

and roared down toward us, thin little darts of flame spitting from his guns. When he had passed, he turned and came in from the rear. Another burst.

Then something stabbed and burned across my left index finger. I saw my blood start out across it in all directions, but I could tell at a glance it wasn't serious. Then another something seared and cut across the back of my head. I clapped my fingers to the wound and they came away with blood on them. How long would I live? That last wound was the end. I knew it; I felt it as I felt the blood coursing from my body. But that bastard—he would come with me!

Now that bullets had brought blood from my body, they scared me, and because they scared me I wanted to kill as I never wanted to kill before. That bastard kept firing and firing, and I wanted to smash out his brains against those guns with my bare hands.

He was up there again, still in the same position, safe from Huber's gun which he thought was still active, and beyond mine. He was preparing for another attack. This time when he turned upon us, I would turn upon him. If my guns didn't get him I would ram the bastard —he was coming with me!

He swung around to attack and I turned to meet him. Quickly he swerved out of range. Through the static of the broken phones, I heard Huber moan. Maybe I could still get the kid back to the base. But the Jap came back. He began to make another pass at us, and again I turned to meet him. He twisted into a loop, and then back into his former position. He was watching us like a vulture, waiting for me to turn for the clouds so that he could rake us again. For a hundred years—my watch must have moved but forty seconds—the game went on. Now he was at us again. I turned like the crack of a whip—I had him in my sights —he was gone with a diving turn. I wheeled for the clouds and, looking back as I entered them, I saw him turn away.

I was flying on instruments—on those that remained. Over my earphones Huber still moaned every now and then. I wanted to get him back. I wanted him to live. How long can the blood of a nineteen year old last when it runs out from bullet holes? The moaning had stopped. I didn't want to look back. The last time I had looked his blood-spattered baby face had made me weak.

I tried to contact Midway, but my set had been shattered to uselessness by hot lead. We were flying blind with little more than a compass to guide us. The clouds were thick, impenetrable. I had lost all track of drift figures and as we flew, longer and longer, the dread and helpless feeling that comes with being lost over the sea began to gnaw at what little spirit I still retained. Now and again Huber mumbled something, but I couldn't make out any of the words through the static and the droning of our engine. What was he saying, this nineteen year old, so close to heaven and so far from home?

I broke through the clouds at regular intervals, hoping to see one of my squadron mates to join on. Neither Midway nor even a landmark to Midway was in sight. There was just sea, broad and blue and endless. The gasoline would give out soon.

Then, *there was a reef!* It was Midway. I began to flash recognition signals so they would know it was a friend that was coming in. I came lower and lower— when all at once I came to the bitter realization that here was not Midway but either Hermes Reef or Kure

Island. If it was the Pearl and Hermes Reef we didn't have·enough gas to reach Midway. There was no choice to my guesswork. I flew on the supposition that it was Kure—if only it *was* Kure Island!

It is fifty-five miles from Kure to Midway and I flew those fifty-five miles, and when I was through Midway was not there. I had been wrong in my reckoning, fatally wrong. Half in hysteria I began to execute left-hand turns, trying to figure where I was. There was no reason to it, but nothing had reason any more. The gas would soon run out. It was running out now. Soon the motor would sputter and stop.

I was in another of those wild left turns when I felt Huber kicking the rudder bar in a righthand direction. I didn't want to look back at him, but I had to. Mutely and with feeble gestures he pointed to port, to what appeared to be nothing but a black cloud hanging over the water. It looked as if it might be a burning ship, but it would be a good idea to land close by. There would be life-boats down there. I headed toward the black smoke.

Just then a pair of Army Flying Fortresses swept by. I wanted to yell Hallelujah! That was the way I felt. I moved in behind them. They knew the way to Midway and in just a few minutes there it was!

Smoke was still columning up from it in several places. I spiraled down for a landing, when all at once I discovered that the shattered hydraulic system made it impossible to lower the wing flaps to break the speed when we approached the ground. I was getting ready to climb up again to lower the flaps with an emergency manual control, when Huber mumbled again.

Damn the flaps to hell!

We touched ground at high speed, bounced up into

the air again, bounced down again, blew a tire, and after rolling a good distance we stopped. Field men dashed toward us, with a stretcher. Gently they lifted Huber from his seat. He was still conscious when they carried him away.

"Do you think he's got a chance?" I asked one of the men standing by.

The man shrugged. "Maybe; maybe not."

I was returning from the dressing station when I saw Jesse Rollow coming toward me. "Jesse," I called out, "how many got back?"

He fell in beside me. "I don't know, Tom," he replied in a shocked, toneless voice. "I just got back myself."

We lit cigarettes and stood watching the sky, waiting for friends to come home.

10. *The Battle Goes On*

They came back—some of them. One by one, at irregular intervals they appeared, emerging from a hum in the far-away sky, unidentifiable at first, then growing larger and larger until they took shape and form. And when they landed, one by one, we ran forward to greet our friends, shaking their hands with an eagerness that was strange to us.

About eleven o'clock there was another alert. Our planes, the ones that could fly again, needed gas and bombs. We didn't have time to prepare them now so we headed for shelter. An engine roared near by. We looked and saw a lone fighter taking off. That sight filled us with pride and remorse. Pride, because he was one of us going against he knew not what, going alone in the face of any odds; remorse, because it was only then that we realized how badly our fighter squadron had been hit. A few minutes later the all-clear sounded, and we emerged from the shelter to see part of a Navy dive-bombing squadron coming in to gas up. They were followed by the lone fighter plane. Captain Marion E. Carl stepped out of it looking slightly disappointed.

For a long while we survivors waited together on the field—we were now twelve—listening for the sound of more engines in the sky. Now and again we thought we heard another, but it was only a mirage of sound. And finally, when many silent hours had passed, someone looked at his watch. . . .

71

And then we all walked away.

Major Henderson, Gil Schlendering, Maurice Ward, Tom Gratzek, Dick Blain, Bruce Ek, Paul Hagedorn, Albert Tweedy. They would not fly back any more.

As we walked toward the command post to make our report, Dick Fleming shook his head.

"Eight out of sixteen," he stated to no one in particular.

Another group of dive bombers led by Major Ben Norris had made a successful attack on a Jap battleship, but as yet we hadn't checked their losses.

Rollow and I went back to the dugout while a list was compiled for a night attack. Our dugout that was so small and cramped grew suddenly cavernous. The empty bunks were mute reminders of Ward, Schlendering, and Major Henderson. Jesse and I didn't have much to say to each other. When we did speak, we spoke of the battle that was still going on between our Naval craft and those of the Japanese. The runways had not been bombed. Obviously the Japanese were planning to invade us and to land their own planes upon those runways. All that we could do now was wonder at the outcome.

Dick Fleming stopped by and told us that there was a rumor current that Schlendering had been picked up by a PT boat and taken to a hospital on another island. One-third of the heavy cloud that filled our room shattered. Perhaps it was true. Perhaps Gil was safe. I tried not to excite myself at the thought. Seeing what we had seen, it did not seem very probable that such good luck could befall anyone—not when it was known that the Japanese would machine-gun anything they saw in the water, living or dead.

72

And then another piece of good news burst upon us. A medical orderly brought word that Huber would live.

In the evening the names of those who would participate in the night attack were posted. My name wasn't included because my plane wasn't in shape to fly. I was ordered to assist in the runway lighting detail for the take-off and landing operations of the flight. Of the remaining pilots in the squadron, ten or twelve were listed to participate in the attack. Major Norris would lead this group.

This time when we were gathered in the ready tent receiving instructions for the flight, I tried to memorize the faces of those who went out. There was a different set to the boys. The old look of tension had been replaced by a newer one. It was not a look of resignation but something like that. I don't know how to describe it.

When the instructions were completed the flyers walked to the planes, climbed in, tightened the chin straps of their helmets, pulled their goggles down over their eyes and then, one by one, they taxied out onto the runway, into the wind, and then with a roar each plane raced upward into the night sky. I watched them until their flaming exhausts passed from sight, wondering who would not return.

Back in the dugout, Rollow and I decided to try to get some rest. I climbed up into Schlendering's bunk. All that had happened during the years before burst upon me in a wave of fatigue that was so throbbing I could hardly bring myself to close my eyes, far less go to sleep.

I called out to Rollow but he didn't answer. I presumed he was asleep. A silence so loud it was earsplit-

73

ting filled the room. I felt lonely, terribly lonely. I wanted to get drunk, riotously stinking drunk. Then thoughts—all kinds of thoughts arrived to keep me company.

There was a dull explosion, loud enough to shock me to attention. A moan was rising, rising to a climbing scream. The shell was coming straight for us!

"Rollow! Hit the deck!"

In a flash of time we were both lying face down on the floor. The shell whistled over our heads and exploded deafeningly near by.

We stood up. I looked at Rollow and Rollow looked at me. My mouth felt as though it were lined with a blotter.

"Well," I said finally, "we have visitors."

"Yeah. They're here all right. What are you going to do?"

"Well," I replied with no attempted humor, "I'm going to take my .45 with me up on the back porch and watch them come. I don't care for a rice diet."

"Okay, I'll go with you."

So, with pistols in hand, we climbed out of the dugout prepared to meet the invaders. Wake Island, I thought resignedly as I checked my ammunition clip and snapped a bullet into the magazine. Let 'em come!

The island was alive with activity. Seachlights were sweeping over the water and our guns began a steady cannonade. Let 'em come!

A sudden silence. But from the northwest the sound of the sea thrummed like a distant drum. One by one the searchlights went out. All was clear again.

It had been only an enemy submarine that had shelled us—the impudent bastard. I was more or less prepared to die in the air; that was all right in a way, but to be killed in a dugout, killed by a submarine—it sounded like waste and I didn't want to be wasted.

Rollow and I turned in again but we did not sleep. Somehow it just didn't seem like night any more. We forced conversation for a while and then it became time to go out and light the flare pots along the runway. Our friends should be back pretty soon.

Again, one by one, at irregular intervals they came back—some of them. Again there was earnest, sincere handshaking. Again we watched and listened to the sky. Again the nervous glancing at timepieces—each second that ticked away drained off a pint of gasoline and with it drained the chances of return for those still missing. Two planes were overdue: Major Norris and Sumner Whitten. A long half hour later we were told to give them up.

Rollow and I walked down the long runway extinguishing the flare pots. The field became dark again. Then, just as we were leaving, a lonesome hum became audible to me. Was it more imagination? I turned to Rollow.

"Do you hear it?"

He nodded, first slowly, and then as the sound grew louder he shook his head vigorously and grabbed my arm.

"Come on," he cried.

We raced down the runway touching flame to the dampened wicks on the flare pots, and as we ran the path behind us became like a marching roadway of light.

The incoming plane circled once as we stood by. Who would come back! Then he came down bouncing along the landing strip. We ran forward to greet whoever it was that had returned. It was Whitten.

The return of one of the planes presumed lost re-fired our hope that perhaps Major Norris would also come back. We kept the fires burning a long time for him—they are still burning for him in our hearts.

Captain Tyler became our commanding officer.

It was after midnight. I had not slept for twenty-four hours. I could not put from my mind the memory of my friends. They were still too real. I remembered their faces too well. It was not as though they had died after a preliminary illness. There had been no time even to imagine their loss. But they were gone—gone. Damn it all, I couldn't believe it! I just couldn't conceive the truth that not one, but nine men—friends—had passed beyond me in the tiny interval of a day. The night passed, and it was morning again.

There were many empty chairs at the mess-hall table, and not much talk. All the many things we had to say to one another were better left unsaid. No use discussing epitaphs. In the afternoon we would fly again.

The operations officer announced our mission: two Japanese capital ships were within our range; one was damaged, the other sailing a defensive patrol. No enemy aircraft were reported in the area. Therefore, the ships were practically helpless, and the mission would be an easy one. Nothing to worry about but anti-aircraft fire, and the Japanese are cross-eyed, aren't they?

I wanted to go out on this attack. A new code of ethics had been born as of yesterday morning. It was a code that dictated duty to one's comrades. Every man —to remain a man—had to share whatever dangers there were to be shared. That was the only way to keep face and to keep friends from now on.

In the ready tent the attack was diagrammed on a

blackboard and instructions were given. The enemy ships were quite a distance from us, and Captain Tyler ordered that all pilots with damaged equipment were to remain grounded. Then came the command.

"Everybody got it? Okay—let's go."

A new gunner had been assigned to me. He was another youngster. He had stepped from the ranks of a ground crew, volunteered for this action. I did not ask him of his experience or lack of it. His face was so aglow with eagerness and confidence it would have been criminal to embarrass him now.

I checked the plane. It seemed to be in fairly good shape. I was just about to taxi out for a take-off when I remembered the radio and tried it.

"Zed from Moore. Zed from Moore. Give me a short count."

No reply.

"Zed from Moore! Zed from Moore, give me a check, please."

No reply.

"Zed from Moore! Zed from Moore, I am checking. Answer, please."

Still no reply. The radio was dead. I thought of going anyway and then I thought of yesterday, only yesterday, when I was lost 150 miles away without a radio. Already most of the squadron was in the air and Tyler had ordered all planes with damaged parts to remain grounded. I got out, hoping to find another plane that was undamaged, but not a one. I was forced to dismiss my very disappointed gunner and tried to occupy myself until the others came back.

I walked over to Danny Iverson's plane and inspected it. It was in a bad way. He had returned from the first attack with over two hundred bullet holes in it and it was damaged beyond repair. He had come in with only one wheel in landing position; the other was locked by a bullet in its mechanism, but he had landed all right, remaining always on the runway and causing no damage to himself or to the B-17's parked close by.

About two hours later our planes returned. While they were still in the air I unconsciously counted them. There should be ...

One ... two ... three ... four ... five ... How many went out? How many are missing?

Someone had not come back. As soon as they landed we who had remained behind rushed forward to meet them. Captain Armand De Lalio was the first we reached. He saw the question before it was asked.

"Dick Fleming," he replied curtly. "Antiaircraft fire. Instead of jumping he dove down on them and dropped his bombs. It was too late, that's all."

That's all.

11. *Requiem and Recall*

On the sixth of June, Bob Vaupell and I flew out to sea in search of survivors. From the air the water was a stretch of blue that went on and on without end. It looked quiet, hiding the men and the ships that had fought and lost on the day before. I could see the shadows of our wings magnified upon its glassy surface. I could see all these things and mark them, but they had lost the poetry of their meaning.

I was flying Captain Tyler's plane. Kure Island was passing below us when by chance I noticed the oil pool forming at my feet. Obviously an oil line had broken. I turned immediately and headed back for Midway. The engine wasn't going to run for long without oil.

The others found no survivors floating on the sea, but on that day Captain Dick Blain returned to us. He came with the victorious smile of a man who has killed Death. His only reply to our wide-eyed greeting was an immediate call for his favorite breakfast, "Eggs over easy and lots of 'em!" He had spent two days in a rubber boat and he was in no mood for long storytelling.

When Blain came back we thought that perhaps some others would return also, but it might now be said that he was the last and only one.

On the sixth of June, the Battle of Midway was officially declared over. Forty-eight hours later we went back to duty.

The seventh of June was a calm and gentle Sunday. At

ten-thirty in the morning church call sounded and by eleven o'clock a group of about eighty-odd gathered in the open space where the Catholic service was to be held. All about us were the marks of the aerial bombardment. Debris was scattered everywhere. It looked like anything but a holy place.

Father Woloch called me to help him with his vestments. We knew each other well. There had been many times before when Tom Gratzek, Dick Fleming, and I had passed the evening hours in talk with him. Always we had gone to Sunday Mass together, but on this morning I went alone. Father Woloch knew what had happened to them. He knew, too, of what I thought. When I had finished helping him and turned to go back to my place before the altar, he stayed me for a moment.

"Thomas."

I did not look into his eyes.

"Yes, Father."

"Pray for them, Thomas, all of them."

"I will, Father, I will."

The service began. I held my rosary very near as I pronounced the prayers. In the rows of men about me there was a deep reverence. I could hear through the blur of voices many names being mentioned, and I, too, spoke names. It was a small gesture but it was the only one I could make.

When we went back to duty, my detail was not a very pleasant one. I was ordered with Captain Williamson to make an Inventory of Effects of the belongings of Major Henderson. When an airman dies, when any soldier dies, there is not much left to show for him: a few pictures, a few books, some clothes, some letters—worn from constant reading—and that's about all.

Captain Williamson chose the items while I made the inventory:

"One picture—" called Williamson, "a woman."

I wrote: *"One picture—a woman."*

It was a picture of Mrs. Henderson. I had seen him looking at it many times. She was a lovely woman. I remembered her from San Diego.

"One picture—a dog."

"One picture—a dog," I wrote.

It was a picture of Major Henderson's dog, a little black and white terrier. I remember that Major Henderson told us of a trick the dog played whenever a Naval officer came to his house.

"Which would you rather be, a Naval officer or a dead dog?" Major Henderson would ask his dog, and the dog would roll over and play dead.

"Four letters."

"Four letters"—worn with rereading—the last words from home, the words studied and restudied for all the strength of their meaning. I did not know what the letters contained, but I could guess.

"Four books."

"Four books"—technical manuals for the most part. The hours we had reserved for amusement the Major had reserved for more preparation: how to do things better in order that those who served under him might perhaps live a little longer.

"Shoes."

"Shoes"—they were racked in a straight line, well shined, well kept.

"Uniforms."

"Uniforms"—clean, well pressed, all of them.

That was all.

We packed those things and they were forwarded, I suppose, to the "nearest of kin."

I tried not to think that perhaps someday someone would be detailed to make an inventory of my own effects.

We fell back into the old routine. It was pleasant to be flying peaceful patrols again. The days were emptier now as our ranks were emptier. Nothing of consequence happened that I can remember. And then, on the twenty-sixth of June, we were relieved. Flying Fortresses returned us to Pearl Harbor!

12. *Stein Song with Broken Glasses*

"Six Marines were eating beans parlez vous...."
A loud burst of laughter followed. We were in one of the rooms of the Moana Hotel. I wasn't thinking of anything in particular at the time. Perhaps the laughter and pleasant atmosphere made it easy to forget—for a little while, anyway.

I had a full glass in my hand and a host of friends around me. We had been given forty-eight hours of furlough on our return to Pearl Harbor, and we were spending these hours lustily—without shame or apology. We had come from the Naval-disciplined Royal Hawaiian Hotel to this oasis for the sole purpose of escape.

One of the boys was trying to open a Coke bottle with a rusty pocketknife. Somebody muttered the old Marine Corps expression, "Don't do it that way. There must be a harder way." Again we all laughed. Someone else began to talk about what duties we might soon face, but the subject was quickly changed.

Outside I could hear the surf pounding on Waikiki Beach. It is but eight hours as a Fortress flies from all that was Midway to these shores, but again what a long, long cry it was.

Someone broke out in another tune that ended in laughter. Someone again mentioned "duty" and the subject again changed.

The forty-eight hours flew by. I have little else to say of them, little else to remember.

I went back to Ewa Field to report myself ready and

fit to fly and fight again. I was assigned to a new squadron—Marine Diving Squadron 232. Danny Iverson and Bruce Prosser were assigned with me. The new unit was commanded by Major Richard C. Mangrum, a stern-faced veteran Marine flyer. There was something about him that suggested Major Henderson; perhaps it was his we-are-going-to-get-'em expression. As for the others, the squadron was composed mainly of men fresh from the United States, and most of these wore wings less than a few months old.

Yes, I remember how we were on that first day, and I remember, too, how we were not too long afterward. Even in remembering it is difficult to realize just what did happen.

Back to duty. *There is a big job to be done. You are the first line, the very first line. We have got to be the base. We are not playing marbles, you know....* And again the same expressions to spur us on, to shape us into a unit prepared for battle. The same old expressions, and I wondered if in the final analysis it was the beginning of a now familiar story.

Shortly after the squadron was organized we received orders to train for aircraft carrier service—and immediately the quarter-deck lawyers came to the mutual agreement; to wit, we were to be assigned for duty with a carrier.

A section of the field had been laid out to duplicate the area of a carrier's landing deck, and for many days our practice consisted of putting our planes down into that comparatively small space. Then when we were considered sufficiently skilled in this basic exercise, we were told that on the next day we would conduct more realistic maneuvers from the deck of the U.S.S. *Hornet.* Captain Bob Galer who was conducting the bounce drill told me he didn't think I was ready to try it yet. I felt confident and begged him to let me go. Finally he agreed.

The next morning we flew out to the *Hornet*. Larry Baldinus, one of my squadron mates, a flyer who had risen from the ranks, took me as a passenger to demonstrate our first landing. The *Hornet* was sailing only a few miles offshore, and in a little while we sighted her.

Moving into formation for landing, the squadron started down. The carrier became larger but still it seemed not large enough. I looked behind me. O'Keefe, one of my other squadron mates, was flying directly behind us. Our rudder bisected his wings evenly. By the time I turned my eyes forward again I could make out the figure of the landing officer in his white helmet waving a flag as a signal for us to cut our engine. We stalled in, bumping along the deck until we were brought to a stop. We rolled further up the deck and then I turned and saw O'Keefe. He had already cut his engine and was almost upon the carrier's deck when he changed his mind and threw the throttle forward again to climb back into the sky. His plane was moving at a dangerous speed for us. For a moment I was frozen in my seat. I saw the spinning propeller, a veritable sword that could slash a man in half 3,200 times a minute, coming toward me. The plane was careening drunkenly over the decks, O'Keefe fighting to control it. Without willful thought, without anything but automatic motion I bounded clear of our plane to a sheltered place. O'Keefe hit left brake and suddenly his plane swerved to the far end of the deck, wobbled for a moment, and fell overboard. O'Keefe was rescued, a destroyer picking him up. He had been injured slightly, enough to keep him out of the air for several days, but otherwise he was just a little pale and very wet.

On that same day I qualified as a carrier pilot. It was not quite as difficult as I had imagined. The most important things I learned were timing and split-second judgment. It is not a pleasant thing always to be dependent upon a split second, but such is the rhythm of our life. A long second generally means the last. You are not supposed to think about that.

When we returned to the base it now seemed fairly certain that in a very short time we would be moved from the Islands, probably upon a carrier. Everything pointed in that direction. I did not allow myself to think much about it. I went to the movies often.

Sometimes, and only sometimes, friends and brothers separated from each other by the war do meet. Whenever they do, it is, of course, an occasion. And so it was with me. On one very memorable day, in August, an orderly entered my quarters to announce, "There is a soldier outside asking for you, sir. He says he is your brother-in-law." Jimmy! I went outside and there he was, a little huskier, a little older, a little more secured in himself since the last time I had seen him. That last time dated back to my graduation leave.

The differences in uniform and rank in no way detracted from the effusiveness of our greeting. It was good to see him, really and truly good. He was a reminder of things and people that were close to me, and here the sight of him brought those memories into sharp focus.

We exchanged the news from home.

"Janet is getting along fine."

Those words were ever present. There were other things, little things that reached big proportions when they were spoken here—over five thousand miles from home.

I decided I was going to show him a big time. I'd wine him, dine him, and as a sort of special treat I would take him to Lalani village.

Just as these things were going through my mind I heard excited voices outside my door. I poked my head out, but before I could say anything one of the boys said, "Better get your gear together; we're leaving in a couple of hours."

I didn't have to explain to Jimmy. He knew. We shook hands and then we parted. He would write another letter, not the one I had imagined.

An hour later Marine Dive-Bomber Squadron 232 trooped aboard a small carrier and set sail. Once again we were at sea—with no Aloha to soften our departure.

13. *Destination Unknown*

We were at sea—far out at sea. Days were long; each minute, each hour ran its full slow length. Nothing but sea! And the long, gaunt destroyer that convoyed us. There was a brief time in the beginning when a current of excitement about our voyage had spirited us in a small way. We were bound for an unnamed destination, but wherever it was, we knew what we would find there.

I began to write a letter to my wife. I intended it as a last letter. There were things I wanted her to know, things she must know and must always remember, but at the same time there were things she must never know— Each day I wrote a portion of the letter. This is how it began:

At sea.

Dearest Janet,

Once again we are under way. I don't know where we are going but I am sure it is to a safe place, so you must not worry about anything.

I'm really enjoying this trip. There are hundreds of things that keep us occupied, but there is still always time for me to think of you, very much more than merely often.

Just before I left Pearl Harbor I did catch a brief glimpse of Jimmy. He is looking very well. The Army seems to be doing him much good, so tell your dad he needn't be concerned too much. I had a letter from

Mother and she tells me that you are getting along very well. I know Mom. I know she would tell me every-thing was all right just to keep me easy. I will mail a letter to Mother and Dad at the same time I mail this.

I am trying my best to learn to be a father, but it seems so very wonderfully impossible that I don't know how I will ever manage.

I will close here for today. Tomorrow I will con-tinue. . . .

Oliver Mitchell entertained us in the duller hours. His imitations of Jerry Colonna and Bob Hope would have sent a ripple of laughter across anyone's face. He was a natural-born comedian. It was not until a month later that I ceased to describe him as such. We played hearts quite often. We read books. We did anything and every-thing that would cause less conversation and less think-ing of things to come. Every so often the shrill bugle call "General quarters" would ring through the ship and we would stand to our battle stations until the all-clear sounded. Those were tense moments, but all our moments were tense.

I always think of the baby as a boy. How do you think of it? Do you see the doctor often? Are you sure you are taking every care of yourself? I hope you are not alone much of the time. I would give anything to be able to share these months of waiting with you. But this is war, and we all must make our sacrifices—you and I and even the unborn.

The long days went on. Still no mention was made of our destination. We speculated widely. Would it be the Gilberts? Or Guam? Danny Iverson said it was Tokyo.

There was only silence whenever we asked. Some of the younger pilots openly looked forward to our landing. They wanted action. Others, like Charley McCallister and Bob Rose, were beginning to ask more pointed questions of Prosser and Iverson and me. We had been to war. We had attacked and killed, been attacked and almost been killed. They wanted to know what our reaction to all this was. Would *they* be afraid? What could we tell them?

Janet dear, no matter what happens—but nothing will happen—remember me always, because I love you.

The voyage goes on. It is still pleasant, almost a vacation cruise. The only thing missing is shuffleboard.

Oliver Mitchell and I had a standing joke between us. The first one to see the other—and we saw each other often every day—would give as his greeting, "I wonder how it would feel to be twenty-six." Both of us had just turned twenty-five. The twenty-sixth year was still a question.

I think it looks fairly certain now that we will halt at a friendly island and operate from there. Hardly anybody knows anything about these places but some of the crew men who have visited those isles say the climate is languorous and the natives should prove very amusing. I am getting to be quite a Gulliver, don't you think?

Darling, I will continue later. I have just been summoned to the wardroom.

We were all gathered there, the pilots from the fighter squadron as well as our own. The tenseness that had been our mate all through the voyage was with us now as never before. Something was going to be said, something important.

Major Mangrum stood before a table on which a large map was spread. At his direction we huddled about him.

"Well, gentlemen," he said, "this is our destination," and he pointed to a little speck in the southwestern corner of the map. "It is Guadalcanal."

14. *Journey into Fear*

We sailed nautical mile after nautical mile toward the Solomons. I knew nothing of the land that was our destination, nothing except that we would fight there. *Fight*—the memory of Midway defined that word for me. It was a memory that left no illusions of confidence or valor.

Confidence and valor—those were the qualities I wanted for my own. I needed them to light what dark hours would come, but I wanted them no more as illusions. Illusions deserted with the first sounding of alarms. I wanted them to hold so I would not be afraid again.

Most of all I had become afraid of fear itself. I became afraid that when the next zero hour would come I would disgrace myself and, with me, all that I believed. I tried to impress myself with a constant repetition of, "I am not afraid. I'll come back. It's just not possible for me to die—not here—not so far from home," and I almost convinced myself. But every time I seemed halfway there, I remembered those bullets that had found me and touched me, and I fell back again. It took just a tiny piece of steel in any one of a thousand right places for a telegram to find its way back across the world to one Mrs. Thomas Moore:

"...deeply regret to inform you that your husband..."

A tiny piece of steel...

I don't like to remember the struggle that raged in my

brain. It was a nightmare that never ended with the night. I was fighting for my confidence as I would fight for my life. I convinced myself then that I would die. Nothing could avert it. It would be only a question of time, a question of when the piece of steel would find me and end me. That was the best way—be negative. If in some impossible manner I lived, it would be like a surprise, but if I died my end would come as an end to waiting. It would come according to expectation and play, and in the final moment there would be no place in that moment for disappointment.

Perhaps it may be said that this was a clumsy way of thought, irrational and unheroic—perhaps. But it was the only answer for me. If I had continued to mark my time with thoughts of home, of peace again—while each moment I was sure of nothing but the uncertainty of life or sudden death—then I might well have gone mad trying to keep from dying in this scene while groping out for the next.

Before this journey ended, I wanted to talk to a priest. I wanted him to hear my confession and to grant me the sacrament of Communion.

We came to a friendly island. It was midday when we arrived; heat waves blurred across the flight deck and the air we breathed was like the breath of hell. The temperature had reached that degree of Fahrenheit where we greeted each other with a profane comment about the weather instead of "Hi ya," or "Hello."

We anchored in a naturally formed harbor off a small town. The town itself was invisible from the shore but hardly was the anchor secured when liberty parties organized themselves all over the ship. War had not changed this. We were still incurable tourists.

An hour passed, another hour. Still no announcement that we could go ashore.

While we waited I conceived plans of what I would do with my few hours ashore. First I decided I would try to locate a priest, and if I did I would ask him to hear confession and grant me Communion. Then I would buy something to send back home to the family and then, if time allowed, I would go to the airport and look up John Massey who had attended flight school with me. It would be good to see him again. I told my plans to Charley McCallister, and he agreed with my itinerary completely.

"I really would like to see a priest myself," he admitted. "You know, Tom, you never know..."

As some hours passed and still no liberty boats put out from the shore, the lush green shoreline became a bitter frustrating sight. Maybe a priest was there. If it was really under French dominion there would certainly be a priest. The shore was less than four city blocks away—the distance from my mother's house to the subway. I waited and waited all through that day, but when nighttime came I went to sleep thinking of the plans I had made, though trying to forget them.

We were not permitted ashore.

At 5:45 in the morning the sharp, annoying notes of reveille sounded through every amplifier on the ship. I woke to find that we were still at anchor, and through the porthole I could see the shore. We were no farther away from it than yesterday.

The sight refired my conviction that we would be allowed to land. Yes, we would. When mess call sounded I did not respond. We would be permitted ashore, and when we were I wanted to be in the state

94

necessary to receive Communion. But Charley McCallister urged me to breakfast.

"It's no use, Tom," he argued. "After telling us where we're going they won't let us ashore. They probably figure that if a bunch of us get on land somebody is bound to shoot his mouth off and they are not taking any chances on that."

What Mac said was logical. It was a good reason, a very good reason. The presence of American planes in Guadalcanal was planned to give the Japs the same effective surprise that they had given us at Pearl Harbor. It was to be expected that every precaution would be taken to keep it secret. In spite of this realization I decided to remain hungry. I still had faith that we would go ashore and I would see a priest.

About eleven o'clock in the morning my faith was borne out. Liberty parties were officially organized and our entire squadron was given leave to go ashore. I wanted to laugh and tease McCallister with a few passing variations of "I told you so," but he darted into the first launch so fast that I never had a chance to do anything but follow before it pulled away.

When we arrived at the wharf, Mac and I set forth together on a road that ran to the village. It was a half mile to the village, and with every step we seemed to increase the speed of our pace. Every minute counted now. This was our last stop before the Solomons, the last stop until we flew and fought again.

We came to the village. It lay at the bottom of a long hill that swept upward beyond it. It was like the side street of some gasoline stop on U. S. Highway 66.

Perched alongside the dirt road thoroughfare was a ramshackle building adorned on the outside with a few faded signs that gave it the appearance of a general store. We entered to ask directions. The interior of the shop was littered with almost every variety of product unimaginable; empty baling bags and smashed wooden crates limited the space considerably. After a few moments the proprietor came out from behind a partition at the rear of the store. He was a withered little man; dirt and the tropic sun had marked him to the point where it was impossible to distinguish the original coloring of his skin. Even his nationality was lost, his accent suggestive of no nation at all. He told us that we would find a church on the hill.

We were as part of a Van Gogh canvas as we climbed that hill. Under the brilliant blue sky the countryside was splashed with every shade of green, yellow, and clay-brown. Ahead, halfway to the horizon, stood the mission, a huddle of decadent buildings, warped, windswept, and crowned in rugged splendor with a straight, sun-whitened wooden cross.

The sight of that cross affected me. It was a symbol that took the strangeness from an alien land. The cross at St. Mark's is of molded concrete; this one was of hand-turned wood, but the form was the same. A cross is a cross be it of twigs or silver.

When we arrived at the mission we found it to contain a schoolhouse as well as a church, and the fence of the schoolyard bordered the road. Within the enclosure, thirty or forty children played at a variety of games, seeming to join each movement of play with a loud outcry of determination. In the very center of this uproar stood the calm, watchful figure of a nun.

The scene was too interesting and nostalgic to interrupt, so we just stood there at the fence watching the children and waiting for the nun to notice us. When she did, she appeared neither startled nor surprised. She came toward us, a small, graceful young woman, immaculate and refreshing, though her cloth was black and the sun was burning.

"*Que puis-je fait pour vous?*" she asked.

The obvious fact that in a French protectorate the language used was French had not occurred to me. I tried to rally the remnants of a two-year high school language course to explain to her our wish. After a long while, I composed this sentence of explanation and delivered it with great seriousness of expression:

"*Nous voulons à voir le padré pour déscrebir un confession.*"

She mulled the words over in her mind, seeking my meaning. Finally, she smiled; she understood.

She told us that the priest was away and was not expected back for several days. As our hearts fell, she added that perhaps the Bishop, who lived at the top of the hill, would be able to help us. We waited only long enough to thank her and then we started up the hill. We could see the Bishop's house at the top, and when I saw it, I knew the people of this island were poor. The building was in no way equal to the title of the man it housed. In the United States, the house of a priest would be palatial by comparison.

When we came to the house at the end of our climb, Mac knocked on the door with two polite raps. We waited for about half a minute before the door was opened by the Bishop himself. He was about sixty years old, short, and a little bent. He invited us into his house without asking a question. He just said, "Good day. Enter, please." The Bishop led us into his study before beginning conversation. When we were seated, I told him that we had come for confessional. I didn't mention the Communion.

The Bishop was gracious. Though his English was very broken and spoken with French accent and rhythm, he was most considerate. He nodded and beckoned to McCallister to accompany him. While my friend was with the Bishop, I noticed the room. It was decorated in a crude, sacerdotal style. The furniture was not antique; it was just old and worn. Some of the windows were stained, but most of them were frosted, permitting little light to enter. All in all, it did not seem like a pleasant house to live in.

When they returned, Mac said he would wait outside while I was with the Bishop. I then followed the cleric to the tiny confessional. Once we were seated I tried to speak my thoughts in French, but sometimes when I found my knowledge insufficient to translate my misdeeds, I reverted to English. This caused the confession to last a little longer than usual, long enough for Mac to cluck his tongue, wag his head, and say, "Well, well, Thomas," when we emerged.

Since the Bishop had been good enough to hear us himself, I was a little wary in asking him to grant us Communion, but when Mac prodded me I asked. Again the priest nodded, but then, as if suddenly remembering, he asked if we had partaken of food. Mac and I exchanged glances, and I wet my lips before I spoke again. Frenchmen, they said, had uneven temperaments.

"My friend has eaten," I told the Bishop, "but—"

The Bishop exploded. *"Non! Non! Impossible!* I will not grant Communion to him. *Impossible!"*

When I saw that look of dispirited helplessness come over Mac's freckled face, I felt so badly myself that I could not collect a word of French to explain the situation. Instead I gripped the arm of the Bishop.

"Look—the ship," I pleaded. *"Aujourd'hui, nous allons."*

The Bishop's old eyes looked to where I pointed. From the top of the hill the bay was like a bright blue basin, and there, floating quietly at anchor, was our ship. It looked almost like a picture, but the dark gray war-paint that coated our vessel added grimness to the scene. The Bishop looked. He looked for a long time, and when he turned his eyes back to us they seemed sad and kind and gentle.

"I will grant your friend a dispensation," he said quietly. "Come to the church."

15. *Guadalcanal*

Onward we sailed, closer and closer to Guadalcanal. The sun struck back more heatedly with every mile of our coming. From midsummer to August 20 we had sailed and sailed, and then it was over.

"Pilots, man your planes!"

The procedure for our operation had long ago been given and many times rehearsed. This was the sum total of all the voyage. I moved to my plane, checked it; the propeller turned over once, twice, and then it was a blur of whirling steel. I got the signal from the catapult officer and moved up into position. He signaled again, asking me if I was ready. "Ready." Bang, whoof—and away I went. From a standstill to seventy knots in seconds is quite a thrill.

Once in the air we climbed into formation, leveling off at two thousand. I flew in Number 3 position, behind and to the right of Major Mangrum. It was a hundred and fifty miles to Guadalcanal, but time and the distance sped as our planes sped, and then—Guadalcanal!

There it was. At first it appeared only as a chain of mountains rising jaggedly from the sea, but as we came closer and still closer, I could distinguish its lowland— a few bald hills retreating from the mountains, passing into a huge flat upon which palm trees grew close and tall. Near the water the trees ended sharply to form a wide clearing. That was the airfield. Major Mangrum gave our section the breakup signal and pulled away.

I followed him quickly on a carrier interval. We were

above the field now, starting to circle. Below, a handful of marines were jumping and waving excitedly at us. I lowered my wheels. I lowered my flaps, cutting speed. The field was rough. As my wheels connected with it I relaxed my body for the bumping that would come. . . .

I had landed—the second Marine pilot to arrive in the Solomons.

I have sworn never to forget that moment when a platoon of riflemen surged upon the field to greet us. For two weeks—ever since they had stopped the presses of the world with their attack and occupation of this enemy-held land—they had faced reprisal after reprisal by Japanese airmen. They had stood upon this ground helpless but defiant with little but their fists to shake at the sky. Now we had come. And to them we were a promise—long made, long awaited and at long last kept.

Many hands reached out to help me from my seat. And when I arose I could see beyond them to faces and to eyes. Many of those eyes were filled with tears. The first one to offer his hand when I hopped off the wing of my plane was Bob Miller, the A.P. correspondent. He wanted to know where I was from. I told him and he said, "That's a good story—Brooklyn to Guadalcanal."

There were things to be done and done quickly. With the help of a volunteer ground crew, we stored our planes in places selected for their safety. This accomplished, an infantry officer guided us to a little rise of ground in the center of the field. There the Japanese had constructed a little pagoda which made a perfect operations center for us. I could not understand the smile of pride on the officer's face as we reached it. But then, as we mounted the little knoll, I could see that reason in letters two feet high—a wooden signpost had been nailed to the frame of the structure, and scrawled in bold, clear letters were the words:

"Henderson Field."

There had been no facilities made for our coming, and when night came we prepared to forage what we could for our needs. There were no tents to sleep in, just a canvas shelter that stood on poles and was exposed on every side to the weather. The floor was the damp ground. At about ten o'clock we turned in, wrapping ourselves in flimsy cotton blankets. These were some of the spoils of war taken from the enemy.

Mosquitoes came with the night, mosquitoes almost as big as moths. I had not brought my mosquito netting, and for a while I endured their vicious raids with little complaint. I didn't want to invade the privacy of anyone else's netting, but it became too much. Discretion won out over valor, and I moved myself under Danny Iverson's canopy because I thought he would be the last to object.

Everyone was asleep. Only the buzzing of mosquitoes, the quick patter of a rat's feet, the shush, shush sound of a crawling lizard, a grunt or snore were audible. I thought a few thoughts, and then I, too, fell asleep.

A *smash of thunder!*—but it wasn't thunder. It was an artillery sound, a big artillery sound. Danny sat up with a start. For the first time he noticed me planted no more than an inch from his face. His mouth flew open, and I still don't know whether it was from the shock of the sound or from the sight of me. But before he could speak, another explosion, and another. It seemed as if everyone was awake. A babble of voices broke out almost on me. Someone was grinding at a cigarette lighter before a curse and a shout did away with that threat.

There was a long-drawn-out wailing.

Someone yelled, "Duck!"

We all ducked. There was a deafening explosion not far away.

A shaky voice: "Hey, they're not fooling."

Bruce Prosser's voice: "Take it easy. We'll never hear the one that gets us."

Danny, Bruce, and I had been through this once before and we had little to say. The cannonading was coming from the north, probably from some enemy ships that had made their way into Sea Lark, the northern channel, just for the purpose of shelling us.

We were ordered to remain as we were. The absence of night-flying facilities, the lack of gasoline in the airplane tanks, and the absence of pumping equipment dictated that course. It was not very pleasant to lie there sheltered by no shelter at all, trusting that the enemy would not hit us. I found myself considering the mathematical percentages of the effectiveness of this type of bombardment. Then the sound of the gunning seemed to die off, and there was comparative quiet again.

I lay back trying to return to sleep. If any of the others was still awake I did not know of it. I waited and listened for the sound of the guns to break out again, feeling, somehow, that those first firings had not been a token gesture. And I was right. Those guns had been but a prelude to what is now called the Battle of the Tenaru River. I didn't have long to wait and listen. Again a shell went screaming toward our lines, and before it exploded our bivouac was suddenly awake. The shell exploded and the ground shook. I know that some of us remained shaking after that.

103

"For the love of Mike," someone blurted out.

"What the hell is this—Orson Welles?"

"Those dirty bastards sure can make a lot of noise."

"Why the hell don't you shut up? Whoever told you to tell it to the Marines must have had rocks in his head."

"Damn it, I'm scared and I'm not kidding."

"Whose got an empty pocket, the guy's scared."

"Shut up, shut up, will ya!"

Suddenly above the gunfire you could hear now the sharper sounds of machine guns, now and again the crisp short notes of rifle volleys. The sound advertised what was happening: Japanese were attempting a landing. We became quieter as this realization came to us. More than one hand reached out in the darkness to touch reassuringly the cool barrel of a .45. We would need them if the Japs broke through. In the meanwhile, there was nothing to do but wait and trust that our comrades would hold.

Time after time I found myself dozing, wobbling on the brink of sleep. But then a ton of crashing steel, or a stuttering burst from a machine gun—even the brittle report of a rifle—would startle me back to alarmed wakefulness. I did not mind the firing so very much. It was a message that our troops still held, and "gave proof through the night that our flag was still there."

When morning finally came the battle had all been ended. Only seldom now did a rifle crack out and when it did a long rattle of machine-gun fire would reply, and then that rifle would be silent. Indeed, all would be silent until another single shot would be heard. A machine gun fired again. Silence again. Charley McCallister woke up and heard us discussing the shelling and gunfire during the night. He wanted to know what

104

shelling and what gunfire? He had told us before he was a sound sleeper. Now we believed him!

Word came through to us that the battle had ended in a smashing victory for our side. Around eight hundred Japanese soldiers had been killed during the night and were piled in grotesque heaps upon the beach. What firing we could still hear was only the futile sound of a few enemy infantrymen who were making nuisances of themselves by sniping until they, too, were dead.

Breakfast was offered by our cook, Sergeant Gruenke. It consisted of one main course: coffee. I could see now there was more than a mileage difference between Midway and this forsaken place. Nonetheless, it was good to complain about such little things. It took our minds from the big ones. At least sometimes it did.

Late in the morning Major Mangrum ordered the formation of a flight to search out the ships that had fired at us during the night. He would lead it himself, and I was one of those he chose to participate. We flew out, making a wide sweep of the ocean, but neither I nor anyone else saw anything of consequence. When we returned Henry Hise, one of my squadron mates, made much of his disappointment. Apparently he had expected that we would see at least half of the Imperial Japanese Navy helpless beneath our wings. At least that was the way it should have been. Indeed, in his loud protestations it appeared to me that he considered the whole thing to be a sort of great shame. That was not odd; there had been a time when I thought the same way. But he would learn. For my own sake as well as his I hoped the lesson would not demand too high a price.

For several days there was little activity. Sometimes a few salvos of gunfire would drift down from the hills where our ground forces were constantly engaging the enemy, and very regularly a submarine would surface during the night hours to lob a few small shells at us. But aside from this, our own operations were quiet. So with the time on my hands I visited what places of interest the island afforded; namely, "The prisoners' stockade," where I could listen to the mumbo-jumbo conversations of the miserable little men from Tokyo; also the Lunga River where we could bathe, or the tent of some friend where a card game was generally in progress. Oliver Mitchell would occasionally stroll up and say, "Let's go down to the drugstore for a hot chocolate and a hamburger."

Had I known the island better I would have been aware that this lull was the exception rather than the rule. But it was just as well that I didn't, for soon the lull was broken.

Shortly before midnight a force of enemy destroyers arrived at the northern part of the island, and by the time the news reached us the enemy was involved in a landing operation under cover of a barrage. We could hear the distant firing, and as we did I tried to observe the effect upon those near me. Tonight we would certainly counterattack, and for most of them this would be their first engagement.

No one showed signs of anything that could not be expected. Some talked more and some talked less. While we waited for orders to take off, Oliver Mitchell still made jokes with his Jerry Colonna dialect, but his light-heartedness did not fool me. Oliver-last-minute Mitchell had confided to a friend that he never expected to leave the island alive. And as I watched him the recollection

106

of those words took the sharpness from his attempted comedy. Pagliacci! Thinking of him in that new light took my mind from thoughts of myself. It was not until Major Mangrum ordered, "Man your planes!" that I remembered myself, but it was too late. Now there were things to do.

It was my first night attack. As we flew, a cold moon silvered the black sea. I thought vaguely of that first night flight at Miami. How long ago it seemed! It was really less than a year—the city had been bright with lights of peace. The sky had been velvety and star-filled—how long ago. . . .

"Stand by. Approaching target."

The sky looked cold and the sea still colder. I shivered a little. My mind felt dull. I checked with Hallyburton, my gunner.

"Okay, Hallyburton?"

"Okay, sir."

It would not be long now. . . . Enemy destroyers off the port bow! . . . Attack! I started down, and the wind began its shrill whistle as it tore past us.

A destroyer was down there, a naked silhouette in the moonlight. Little red lights started to dance all over it —antiaircraft fire. . . . The ship grew larger, larger. . . . Another moment, another moment—now!

I hit the bomb release and the bomb fell free. I pulled back on the stick.

Hallyburton did not record the result. "Miss . . ." he said, laconically.

I looked back. I could not hear the explosions of our bombs but I wanted to see them. There were a few flashes from A.A. fire exploding through the sky, not enough to worry about. I saw the exhaust flares from a plane flying near me, and I fell in beside it.

107

Then we came back.

When all were counted one plane was missing—Oliver Mitchell. There was no mention of his name that night, but the price had been paid, at least a down payment.

16. *Attack! Attack! Attack!*

The siren began to wail. A long, long, screaming, rising and falling sound. We started to run for the fox holes. It was an air raid and enemy planes would soon be coming. Already the fighter squadron had taken off to intercept them. Like everyone else, I lit a cigarette—it would steady my nerves—and prepared to watch from the ground sudden death in the high sky. I had never been under an air raid before. This would be a new experience, one which I could watch and record among the other experiences that I never wanted to remember.

The Japanese planes came into view. They were flying high, at about twenty-five thousand feet, in strict, even formation, forming an enormous V. Still higher flew the escort fighter planes, hardly visible at the extreme altitude.

There were our own planes coming! Fewer than those of the enemy but they were flying to attack in a brave little group. They were closing the gap. All at once our planes broke formation and merged into the same space as the enemy. It was hard to see. The sun glared and sweat ran down under the weight of my steel helmet.

A plane began to fall like a bird with broken wings, tumbling over and over and over, down toward the earth. And now as it came into closer range I distinguished its markings. It was Japanese. Hallelujah!

Now another and another and still another plane

tumbled down! They were not all Japanese. In the sky, the bomber formation, not so many now, came on.

Bombs away. They came hurtling down toward us with a screaming sound that ended in a tremendous explosion. Debris flew in all directions. An oil tank was hit and burst into a flame that ran along the ground. One of the shacks suddenly disappeared in a cloud of smoke and a burst of thunder. My face was very close to the sides of my shelter. It was a hell of a place for an airman to be in.

Our ground guns had opened fire. They threw black ink blots against the sky, bracketing the enemy. Suddenly one Japanese plane in the formation seemed to blow up into nothingness. Just as suddenly another started down. It dropped like a sky-writing plane leaving a long black line behind it; it plunged lower and lower and lower. Now I could hear the thin sharp whistling of the wind against its wings. Suddenly it crashed on a hill with one dull boom, and smoke again piled upward from it.

A man had been in that plane. An enemy, but a man, and all that was left of all he had been was a long black streak against the morning sky. Soon even that would be gone with the wind.

Another night. Captain Fletcher Brown, Captain Bruce Prosser, and I took off to attack enemy surface craft. Once in the air, Prosser and I moved into position on both sides of Captain Brown. As always we flew without lights and marked our distance from each other by the cold blue fire spurting from the engine exhausts.

We flew for about seventy-five to one hundred miles to the area where our targets were supposed to be. In that distance we saw nothing. It was an easy flight, almost a pleasant one. Perhaps I was searching too long or perhaps I was thinking too long; for when I turned, the guiding sparks that identified my companions were suddenly missing. There was nothing in the sky but the blackness of the night, broken only by a lantern-like moon. I turned and climbed, hoping to see them again. For an endless thirty minutes I searched through the air in a fifteen-mile radius, but it was all to no avail. Flying with Prosser and Brown, I had not paid as much attention to the navigation of the flight as I should have, and there came to me the awful feeling of being lost in a place that had always seemed lost from all the world I had known. Through some mental gymnastics I finally arrived at a course to follow, relying as much upon hope as upon my compass.

For a long time we flew. Hallyburton was watching for the others while I tried to orient myself from the occasional scattered blobs of land below.

We didn't say much. There was not much to be said. He realized full well the position we were in. Still we kept flying. Soon it must be morning and then the gas tank would be empty. And then—

Keep calm, keep calm. Always remember that. George Waldie had once told me those words. Now was the time to heed them.

Suddenly, there below me was the outline of a destroyer! I tried to identify it by mentally comparing it with the photo silhouettes we had gone over so many times in San Diego. From my position this was practically impossible. One of my greatest fears has always been bombing one of our own ships. I thought it over for a moment and tried to raise the base by radio but my set was on the fritz, and I couldn't contact Henderson Field. Then I decided it must be a Jap as we

111

would have been cautioned had any of our ships been in the area. I decided to attack. I flicked on the inter-communication switch.

"Hallyburton."

"Yes, sir?"

"There is a Jap ship down there. We're going to attack."

"Yes, sir."

Good boy!

Bomb armed. I started down. They must have spotted us. I waited for their antiaircraft fire to begin. Still lower. She was rushing up fast. I'd blow that bastard to kingdom come. Bomb armed. My hand moved to the release.... Now!

I pulled back. The sea rolled back beneath me again. I was on the horizon. I dipped my wings in a gentle turn and looked back anxiously. Seconds went by. The bastard was still steaming along peacefully, with not even a splash to show me how far off I had been. He didn't even open up with the expected antiaircraft barrage. I felt certain then that my bomb had not released. I checked with Hallyburton. He had seen nothing either. This Jap was a cute apple. He figured there must be other bombers near so he held back his fire not wanting to attract them.

I decided to go around and try again. Once again I started down. They could hear me coming almost as loudly as I could hear myself. She was coming up again—damn it, why didn't they fire! Again I had her lined up for a possible hit. In another few seconds that destroyer would be dead. Bomb armed?...Bomb armed.... My hand was on the release.... Not yet—now!... My left hand pulled back on the manual bomb release and the thumb of my right hand mashed the button of the electrical release on the stick.

I pulled up again and turned, hoping to see her blown to bits. But there was no report and no fire. Something must be wrong with the releasing mechanism. There was nothing to do now but to try and get home as quickly as possible and report it.

It was hopeless. We had been flying almost into the morning and still no sight of the base. Very soon now the last drops of gasoline would trickle into the carburetor and burn, and then.... I glanced at my watch. It must have stopped. The hands still stood at 3:30 A.M. I put it to my ear. No. It was still ticking! We had time, lots of time. It was like a reprieve. I knew I had enough gas to fly until daylight and then I could surely locate myself.

An hour later I sighted a pin point of light and went down to investigate. Lower and lower and then I made it out. It was a burning flare pot. It was the field.

When I landed I reported my attempted attack and several planes took off to hunt for the destroyer. They found that "dumb dora," as I termed it, but when they attacked she let loose with a hellish reply of antiaircraft fire. Although our planes tore it to pieces, when they returned that night Major Mangrum added to his report of the action:

"One of our aircraft is missing."

Another afternoon. Navy patrol planes which were now working closely with the aerial force of Guadalcanal, reported sighting a Japanese flotilla composed of a carrier, transports, and destroyers. It was a big order. Every available plane in the squadron took off for the attack, and, Major Mangrum had been doing a lion's share of the work, but once again he chose to lead us.

We took off into a threatening sky, our engines loudly beating our advance. As always I heard the dull throbbing of the senses within me accented by the imminence of battle. I was keyed to high pitch. I could feel the paleness in my face.

Now the distance between ourselves and the enemy was closing. It would not be long now. Minutes perhaps.

Great billows of fog were rolling slowly about. More than a squall was threatening. We flew on. Suddenly we came to a huge mountain of cloud that stretched almost from the sea itself to an altitude very high above us. It was impossible to get through that wall of cloud that looked like a gigantic smoke screen. Perhaps a single plane could break through, but if we flew together it would be suicide. One plane would crash against another and no one could tell how far was the end.

Major Mangrum ordered a change in course and the squadron followed him in search of a break in the wall. We flew for almost a half hour looking for some opening however small, but no luck. That wall was really solid. Those Japs knew how to take advantage of the weather. Major John Smith was leading a group of Grumman Wildcats as fighter protection for us. They were flying high above and to our right. It was good to be able to glance up there and realize that no Zeros were going to catch us by surprise. I heard Major Mangrum call Major Smith. "How does it look up there, John?" And the reply, "Plenty of soup, Dick."

There was no break-through possible. And very reluctantly, Major Mangrum led us back to the base.

Another morning. Word had come through that Japanese troops were effecting a landing at a beach some fifty miles distant. We must attack again. We hoped that we might get the job but it was turned over to the fighter squadron.

The rains came. They fell for two days and two nights, muddying the runways to the point where no operations were possible. We were imprisoned in our tents. There were no movies or dances. There was nothing to do but play cards and talk and wait for the hour when news from home was short-waved to us.

I wrote a letter to Mother and Dad.

17. "Airman, Airman, Where Do You Fly Tonight? . . ."

The rains ceased to fall. The sun burned down from a cloudless sky, the muddy field dried to dust, and we went up·to fight and bomb again. Now there was little time for rest. The enemy flew, sailed, surged, and rolled against us as regularly as the tide. Always we could hear them. By day and by night they came. Air raids, artillery barrages, cannonading from the sea. Gunfire, always there was gunfire, whistling, wailing, and screaming. The ground beneath our feet quaked and recoiled from the thunderous explosions. And if for some minutes there was no sound at all, then the crisp report of a sniper's rifle would crack out.

Through all this there still was an interval in every day when things that once had measured our life came back to us vividly. At 19:00 hours, Guadalcanal War Time, Don McCafferty's little portable radio would rid itself of foreign voices, and Station KNX, Los Angeles, would come through the tiny speaker with a résumé of the news at home. Just the unaccented voice of that American announcer broadcasting to the "swing shift" workers of California would make us feel closer to all that was home. Through air raid and cannonade that voice continued, and though the distance traveled was wide, in that brief quarter-hour the union of home and front became complete. Then, when the voice faded and only cannonading continued, a cloud of loneliness would press down upon us that was not

116

dispelled till someone told a worn-out joke and we all laughed again.

It was on Labor Day, I think, when another of those "desperate journeys" took place. Our losses were mounting. Now, when we flew, almost every flight element was composed of planes and men from part of a recently arrived Naval Dive-Bomber Squadron as well as our own. And that was why on this mission it was Ensign Hal Buell who flew beside me in Colonel Mangrum's lead section. We were going out to attack the enemy by bright moonlight. Four Japanese destroyers had been reported in the area moving in on us. Four destroyers and many Japanese troops. That was the target for tonight.

There were many stars in the sky. A poet might have described it in many words. The flight report described it more directly: *Visibility—clear*. No mission is a time for reflection, but on this night I did steal a moment, maybe more than a moment, to wonder at the sky and to remember that but a year ago—exactly a year ago, on Labor Day—Janet and I had been dancing. But tonight was tonight, not a year ago. Tonight was for bombardment.

Colonel Mangrum was first to sight the target. With no excitement in his voice he reported to the base: "Sighted enemy. We're going in now."

The destroyers had spotted us. Already a few salvos of A.A. fire were clawing the air about us, estimating our position. Their shells were exploding like rocketing meteors above and below us—and those stars were not neutral! The warships were outlined sharply by the moon. They started avoiding action, weaving and crisscrossing, leaving silvery irregular wakes behind.

The burning exhausts of Buell's plane described a

117

downward arc. He was banking, awaiting my movement. I was watching and waiting for Colonel Mangrum to go over in his dive. I intended to follow him quickly as the A.A. was bursting pretty close. Colonel Mangrum went over sharply.

I kicked left—left rudder, left aileron—and we went over on our side. Stick forward. The nose dropped. We began to dive. Below, on the destroyer's deck, the A.A. guns flashed desperately. The sharp whine of racing wind was in my ears, but I didn't hear it then. My hand was on the bomb release, my eyes strained forward to the sight. She was coming up fast and clear. We were on target, on, on, bomb checked.

Now!—*damn it to hell!*

Back, back, back on the stick....

As soon as we were out of the dive I dipped my wing and looked back. In a moment the bomb would explode. The ship was so very clear and close, and then—

Boom!

A column of flame streaked skyward directly from amidships. Everything was lit by the glare. Even then Buell's bomb was on its way down. In a second—

Boom!

Again flame and concussion. All her A.A. guns ceased firing, and the air about us became calm again. Below, the burning of that ship seemed so strange as to be unreal. I could see it, every bit of it, with the fire racing up and down the steel hull. Down there men and a ship were dying, but because no sound of it came through to me the picture impressed me no more than a silent newsreel. I started back for Henderson Field.

When we landed we discussed the attack. It had been a good night. Three of four enemy destroyers had been hit badly. It was a big thing to put an end to. At H. Q., Colonel Mangrum, Major Fletcher Brown, Lieutenant Charley McCallister, and Don Rose congratulated me as though I had just scored a home run with bases loaded. Several others who had heard what had happened stopped me on my way to my tent to pat my back and add to the satisfaction that was now rising like a mountain beneath my chest.

It was not till I was almost entering the tent that I became truly aware of what had happened. The scene I had witnessed kept repeating itself: That destroyer. That mammoth explosion as its twelve hundred tons of steel were torn to nothingness. The thousand tracers spearing upward. If we had been impaled on just one— and they had been so many and so close.

But I'd come back. That was the main thing. A miss is as good as a mile, they say. Bullets don't hurt till they get you, and when they do there isn't much time left for them to hurt. That was what they said. But some- where in those words there was a fallacy. Every bullet hurts, especially the ones that miss. They're the ones you never forget.

I lay upon my bunk trying to relax. Waves of fatigue throbbed painfully through my head. I tried to sleep. I must sleep. Near by several boys were talking. Their voices sounded dull and distant, but presently I heard one say some words that rang in my ears:

"Look, when your number's up, it's up, and there's no two ways about that."

"That's foolish," another answered. "What do you mean 'When your number's up'?—the way you talk makes the whole thing sound like a bingo game."

"Well, in a way that's what it is, just a bingo game—"

119

"Oh, cut it out!" someone said with finality. "You sound like Errol Flynn in *Dawn Patrol.* . . . Numbers!"

And then I fell asleep. . . .

I was wearing a clean white shirt and a bright red tie. It was Mother's Day, and I was on my way to Gimbels to buy Mom a present. In my hand I held seventy-five cents—all that. For a long time I had saved, and now my hand was heavy with those savings. I had promised Mom a present. She was expecting it.

At the corner of Forty-sixth Street and Tenth Avenue, a very little man with a big belly and a balloon face was throwing dice against a curbstone.

"Want to play?" he asked. "Double your money quick."

"Yes, I want to play."

"Well, here's the dice," he said. "Just roll 'em and win."

I took the dice. They were big—so big I had to hold one in each hand. Then I threw them.

"Seven! Seven wins!" I cried.

The little man shook his head. "That's the wrong number. You lose."

I put down some more of my pennies and threw the dice again.

"Eleven!" I cried. "I win."

The little man shook his head. "No. You lose," he said. "That's the wrong number again."

Again I put down more money from my mother's present. I had to win. I had to! I rolled the dice.

"Three!"

The little man giggled. "That's the wrong number. That's the wrong number. That's the wrong number. Try once more. Try once more."

I tried, I tried, and I tried, and then I had no more

120

money left to buy a present for my mother. I had no more of all my seventy-five cents.

The little man giggled and giggled. "You fool," he teased, "you awful fool! Don't you know that you lose on every number?"

I walked home, tears streaming down my face. How could I explain to Mother that I had no present for her. On the street everyone was carrying a long white box tied with red ribbon. It was Mother's Day. How could I explain? I just couldn't explain.

I climbed the steps to our apartment. When my mother came to the door, she would find me empty-handed. I could never tell her. Never, never. But she would ask. Then I pressed my finger to the doorbell. Instead of a little ringing sound—

The siren screamed its alarm through the night.

August and early September are well marked on my calendar of unforgettable days. The routine continued. All around the clock. One hour was different from another only because the sun moved with them, lighting and darkening the land and the sea, ourselves and the enemy. The orders of the day, of every day, were attack, attack, attack! Our losses—we mustn't think of our losses. Attack, attack, attack! Till you're not there any more to respond.

Perhaps I should make more definite mention of those who did not return. But what is there to say? They were all my friends, in a friendship that can neither be accounted for or explained. Like steel, it was tempered by flame. But they ended so often, and with suddenness. When those things happened, I forgot. I forgot it fast. What was I expected to do—cry? No one has that many tears.

The Japs kept coming. They came like a flood, pouring against our fragile lines in greater and greater numbers. They attacked from the north, from the south, in between, everywhere. Our operations became a succession of shuttle-bombing counterattacks. Shuttle-bombing. It means when you take a load of explosives, fly to the enemy, dump them, fly back if you're able, reload, refuel, and take off again. For how long? I never found out.

It was 2 A.M. The report said it was 2 A.M., but I don't really know. All night we had been shuttle-bombing some enemy transports which were attempting to force a beach-head at the northern end of the island. We were killing a lot of little men that night. It came time to go again. We drank some hot coffee, but there was no time to finish even a cupful. There was no time to eat or sleep or wash. There was time only to attack.

As the report stated, it was 2 A.M. when we were ordered to take off. I remember clearly taxiing into position between rows of flares. It seemed cold—cold, damp, and very dark. The engine thundered steadily, and then as I advanced the throttle we began to race down the field. The tail came up. Now the wheels. We started to climb, up, up—suddenly the engines coughed, caught, coughed again—I grabbed for the wobble-pump. The air-speed indicator was approaching sixty knots—not enough to sustain flying speed—the nose dropped—

I was carrying a bomb—check the bomb!

Switch tanks, wobble-pump! God, here come the trees! . . .

18. *If I Should Die Before I Wake!*

My eyes were open. It was daylight, but all that I could see was the khaki roof of a tent through which the sun cut wherever the bowering palms would give a passage. I was in a forward dressing station. The sharp odor of iodine, a flapping white flag with a red cross, and the impersonal steel cot upon which I lay identified it. For a moment all these newly discovered things drifted in a haze, and then everything became clear, crashing suddenly into focus.

Across from me—there was Hallyburton. He lay so still and deathlike, his eyes closed, his face chalk white and bruised. His clothes were ripped in a dozen places and stained all over with dried blood. But he was breathing. I could hear the uneven sound, a gasping sound, as the air rushed by his throat.

As I watched him I began to feel aware of myself. Of pain. It was a throb, an ache, a bayonet—getting worse, worse, worse—and then I could hardly stand it!

There was pain in my face. It felt torn, really torn! But it was my back. *Damn it, I felt as though I couldn't move my back!* It hurt. It hurt like hell. There was something wrong with me. Better get the doctor. I formed the word with my mouth, but no words came out. I tried harder, harder, harder, until—

"Hey!"—my yell was no louder than a whisper. "Hey! Hey! Hey!"—till a dark-haired orderly in a mud-stained uniform entered the tent.

"Yes, sir?"

123

"What's wrong with me? When am I going to see the Doc?"

"You were kind of banged up all right—you and Hallyburton were out cold when we hauled you out of the plane. The plane was pretty badly cracked up and you had a 500-pound bomb on it. You were pretty lucky. You'll be all right. Don't move around, whatever you do. The doctor'll be here soon."

"You'll be O.K." It had a forced note to it. *"Lay still. Don't move around."*

Why did he say, "Don't move around"? It meant my back. He meant, "Don't move around because your back may be serious," and if I moved around—*my back was broken!* The damn fool didn't think I knew it, but I did. Hell, I could feel it.

How long did it take to die with a broken back? A few minutes, an hour, a few days? I saw a picture once with Ann Harding and somebody. The somebody had a broken back. He lived for a day or so. But right there in the picture it said you can't live with a broken back.

I'd die. Soon I'd die. The sweat poured out from my face, but I was cold with a cold I'd never felt before. This was it. In a little while something inside of me would happen and all my life would be over. How much time now? Minutes were going by. I could hear them passing, ticking from my watch. That pain, that damned insistent pain! It didn't get better, it didn't get worse. It was just there. Think. Think of something, anything. Think of Janet.

Janet. I couldn't remember her face. But try, try hard, little by little. Her hair, that came back quickly. It was dark, not short, not long, but soft, fluffed with waves, gentle soft waves. Her eyes, so large and blue and wonderful. Her mouth, soft and full. Her nose, pert

124

and freckled and Irish. Now she was clear. Now I could see her as though she were right beside me. I could even remember her voice, and especially the way she used to say—"Tommy."

It was September. The baby would be born soon, our baby. . . . My back—I became accustomed to the dull ache. I had to go on thinking. . . . My son—it would have to be a son—he would be me, and nothing would ever change that. So, for how long I'll never know, I lay upon that torture wheel, turning it against myself, to hurt myself, to find peace for myself.

I prayed. I prayed with prayers I'd been taught and I prayed with some of my own. I had much to ask for, and I wanted all that I asked.

I wanted a reprieve. Not for a lifetime, perhaps that was impossible. But a little while, just a little while to tell the things I had to say, things that ripped through my mind. I had to tell my mother and my father what it meant to me to be their son. I had to tell them that I full well remembered and make some statement of appreciation of what they had done for me. And Janet. There were so many things that she must know. Words, words, words running like the sea. If only she were here to listen. If only I were there to tell her—the prayer went on. And as I spoke I wondered if God could come this far to hear me.

Time and again I drifted back across the years re-membering little episodes of my life, the pleasant and the unpleasant. It was like judgment day, and this was the review. I couldn't talk, not out loud, because if I did the gashes upon my face would open and blood would flow. Thus I spent the hours reflecting and desiring—things that evolved about a little house at Sheepshead Bay.

Intermittently, almost in punctuation I recalled what the orderly had told me. "You'll be all right," he had said. Maybe I'd be all right. Perhaps—perhaps I would. It was such a wonderful sentence I hardly dared hope for it. Perhaps I'd be all right. Perhaps I'd be all right. I repeated it over and over again. I imagined my back was not so painful now. My face was better except when I moved it. I was feeling better! I was feeling all right! Really, I was!

The flight surgeon arrived sometime later. First he looked at Hallyburton. Was that a good sign? Hallyburton had recovered consciousness. The doctor taped his broken ribs and cauterized his wounds, and by the time he had finished, Hallyburton was smiling.

Then he came over to me. I watched and studied every muscle in his face as he made his examination. I interpreted every movement in every different way, living and dying consecutively, hoping that he would say the right, right words.

He did. He said, "It's O.K., Lieutenant. You'll be O.K."

It is too difficult, it would sound too awkward to describe my feelings through the moments that followed, but I could see nothing through the mist over my eyes.

That evening my squadron mates arrived to visit me. By lantern light I looked at each and every one of them, standing about my bed looking awkward and trying so hard to look casual. They were so few, so very few. Even the little tent was not crowded by their presence.

The words they had to say to me were unimportant in themselves, they had been said for time immemorial by friends in arms at dressing stations around the world. And the stilted smiles to cheer me up. I was glad they had come. Their presence was, in a sense, like being

126

decorated. A real decoration from the most critical judges of all. When I said good-by, to some of them it meant good-by for always—the next day they would fly again.

On the following morning I was taken by ambulance to the airdrome and placed aboard an Army B-17 for transfer to a base hospital. As we waited to take off, I could see from an open gun port a little part of Henderson Field. There was not much to see. Aircraft were being worked over. Not far off a gunner was carefully fitting belts of machine-gun bullets into place, another was welding up little holes that ran through the fuselage. A thunderous roaring overhead—fighters—three by the sound of them, went racing toward the northwest. Today the war was going on again though I was not part of it. That was hard to realize.

The outboard engines on our own plane were started, causing a familiar vibration. Now the inboard were turning over. The fortress began to roll, rolling faster and faster. Then we were in the air. The navigator came by and lit a cigarette for me. As I exhaled a long thin column of smoke toward the roof of the plane, it was as though something else was also passing from me.

Upon our arrival I was taken to the base hospital for treatment of my injuries. After a quick check there I was transferred to a hospital ship that remained at anchor in the bay. My face had been stitched in several places and it was still uncomfortable to talk.

With my transfer to this ship, the very ship itself became symbolic of a rumor that ran the length and breadth of her. It was said that this ship would carry us home soon, and as each day passed and we still remained there, that rumor would be modified with reasons for the delay. But just to talk of home—that magic word—made us all feel better. Home. It meant so many things, almost forgotten things, unbelievably happy things. It meant that autumn was autumn and winter was winter, that spring and summer would also come at their expected times. It meant regular things like dinner at seven and baseball, and eight hours a day and hot water, kids playing on the street, and the sound of trucks and busses and automobile horns. And my family. And Janet.

As the days passed and the ship remained still at anchor in the bay, we began to speculate less on the possibilities of such a voyage. It was argued by some that this ship could never make the trip home. It was not equipped for it, but inwardly all of us preferred to look at her with the eyes of dreamers rather than sailors.

That ship did not sail home. Instead, on one of those days the medical officer made his rounds and examined us for medical classification. When he came to me he seemed in good spirits, teasing me along as he worked. Then with the treatment over he flashed a broad grin. "Get your things together," he said. "There's a ship leaving for the States in a half hour and you're supposed to be on it!"

19. *The Long Voyage Home*

We were going home. We were sailing homeward. *Homeward.* With every moment now we were coming closer to it, lessening the distance from Hell to Paradise. Every time the clock moved we came closer, a moment closer, an hour closer, a day closer. Everything counted. The journey to the rainbow's end could not have seemed longer or more impossible.

We'd never reach home. They'd call the ship back— or today, or tomorrow or the tomorrow after that a torpedo, or a mine, or something would find us and end this dream through which I lived, for always. The more I thought of home, the more I visioned and planned the hours—every hour—I'd be there, then all the more real did disaster become.

This returning was different, very different, from the going. There was a quietness about it. This ship was carrying wounded men from battle and it was so evident upon their faces that if someone had scrawled the word "casualty" across each forehead, it could not have stood out more clearly. Indeed, as I read the faces, it became clear that this returning was not only different but much more frightening than the going.

I didn't walk about too much. It wasn't very comfortable. I spent most of the time in the cabin to which four of us were assigned. We read, played cards and Acey-Ducey. But speech was more difficult still. There was little to be said of casual things that had not been said and repeated, and repeated again. The important things? We sheltered those things close inside us, deep inside, almost hiding them from each other. In a sense we were with our thoughts and dreams like children who will not tell their wishes when breaking a wishbone for fear of losing them.

At times, when we spoke of inane things, on subjects that changed as often as the wind, a few words might be spoken—there were never more than a few—which would cry out a thousand *unsaid* words, important words that would cause me to halt and think and declare.

I was on deck. Upward, near the bow, stood someone with a cane. I greeted him and we talked of the weather and the speed of the ship and breakfast. Then, almost in the middle of a sentence, he interrupted himself and said as if to reassure me, "We'll win this war."

Yes. *We'll win this war.* I swear it in the name of all my friends whose blood has muddied the earth and reddened the sea, *we will win*. The enemy shall submit. The surrender shall be as humble as they were arrogant. We will win this war. We will. They held that faith when they died and their faith shall be kept.

But afterward. What about afterward? There was a chap who was confined to his bed for all the voyage. He would never walk again. He used to lie back upon that bed and stare unseeingly—thinking, thinking, thinking. Because he, too, was from New York, whenever I spoke to him we spoke of the city. It was never much that we said, but then one day he mentioned remembering a man who used to sell apples at five cents apiece at Ninety-sixth Street and Madison Avenue. That man had always worn a faded ribbon in his lapel.

This boy—he mustn't sell apples. He gave his walking, his running, his dancing, and his laughter to give his countrymen a future—and that future must remember him. Upon that pale young face was valor. Even in this grim little room I could see it. How long would that valor last after he came home again? For now I knew why this returning was, for so many, more frightening than the going!

I spent part of every evening in a chair on the starboard side of the deck. There in complete blackness I thought my own thoughts. How far away this was! This ship, rising and falling upon the darkened waters —how different from that morning at Midway and those nights at Guadalcanal and, too, how far from home. But it was good to be here. It helped me to catch up with myself, that I might go forward again. I remembered Oliver Mitchell. I remembered that before he died he'd said, "I don't mind going, but I'd like to know that all this won't end vainly."

I wished that I might have painted a picture for him before he went up to die—a picture that would have shown him what is to come when all this is over. But I could not paint such a picture, because no one had painted one for me. *Is it not time now for it to be said in definite words just how the end will be?* It must be something more than conquest, because I am too little to enjoy that. I am a common man—what will there be for the sons of common men?

This ship with its wounded and tired men was going home. It was one ship and our numbers were not many. If, God willing, our ship came home, then we would be showered with hysterical welcome. But when the

131

war is done—and the armadas return—what welcome will be mustered then?

There were days when the sun burned down almost hatefully upon us and the sea was still and the winds unblowing. There were other days when the rains slashed and the sea roared and the skies shook with thunder. But the important thing was that they were days and they were passing, passing until they became weeks. Until we came close to home.

Then came that morning. We had been so long upon that confining ship and now it was said we would soon land. From early morning we lined the rails but because thick clouds of fog lay heavy upon the water we could see nothing. They told us we were close to the land, but all there was to be seen was the fog, the impenetrable fog. It would have made a wonderful picture, those faces, so different and yet so similar, waiting and watching for a common hope and a common prayer to come into sight.

I didn't see it first, but the man standing next to me did. He made some sound and then his eyes opened wide—very wide. His arm lifted and then—he shouted brokenly.

"There! There it is—it's land!"

The fog had lifted just a little bit, and there it was! We could all see it. A yell went up. Another and another, until all the yells became a cheer. A great long cheer.

The ship sailed on, out of the fog, into the clear.

We were in the bay. There were the buildings. We were home! *Home!* There was land—American land. We were home! *We were home!*

It took about an hour for the ship to reach its berth,

for the lines to be fixed to the land, and gangplanks raised to the sides, for all the things to be done before we became secured.

I walked down the plank. I didn't walk on wood and steel, I walked on air, and then when I felt the *land* beneath my feet, the wonderful, wonderful land, I wanted to put my hand to it, feel it, really feel it.

There were automobiles and people on the street, there were normal, natural things, but I looked and looked at it as though it were all some new wonder of the world. *This was home.* These people walking so carelessly by were my countrymen. I wanted to stop someone. I wanted to stop and tell them how good it was to be back, to be among them again.

I stopped and telephoned. I telephoned Rad Arner. I even remembered his number. It was Edna that answered. She was almost struck dumb when I announced myself. We talked awhile and then I told her to tell Rad to call me at the hospital.

I had to speak to someone close. To Mom. I changed a five dollar bill and dialed long distance.

"I want to speak to Mrs. Thomas Moore in Brooklyn, New York."

I waited for several minutes listening to the operator putting through the call.

I'm home, I'm home, I'm home, I repeated again and again and again, amazed at the wonder of it.

Finally came the words from another operator, "This is New York."

And then they were ringing. A ring. A *pause*. A ring. A *pause*. And then someone picked up the receiver. They cut me off.

"Deposit $4.40 please,"

One by one I dropped the coins into the slot. They

133

clanged and clanged and clanged as they fell—but no louder than the beating of my own heart.

"*Go ahead please.*"

"Hello? Who is it?" my mother asked.

"Hello, Mom! Mom, it's me—Tom. Mom, I'm home!"

"Oh, Tom, you have a son! He weighs nine pounds. You ought to see him."

The past months faded as I stood in the booth. Janet and I had a son!

We who have fought do not asked to be hailed or wreathed for our battles. We ask for something more. We ask for something to come back to. The parade from the insanity of war back to peace is a long march. It is a march that is seldom completed. When a man is put into a uniform and drilled and drilled for war—is regimented, and sent into battle, even when the war is over and the uniform discarded, a little part of him always remains still wearing it.

Vaguely we hear much of ideologies, but because we are at war many of these have retreated into whisperings. All in all they suggest but a world on the move, one way or another. But when the war is over the whisperings will again become shoutings—even ravings!

An army that returns to disillusionment is ready to be recruited to any attractive promise, wild as it may be. If it takes gunfire to obtain it, then gunfire will sound. When one's ears are attuned to it, it becomes easy to imagine it—anywhere—even within our American shores.

Upon that ship, coming home, sitting in the blackness, I hoped for my country—hoped and trusted that it would reply to prejudices and hatreds that must come—reply to them in a way that would maintain the dignity of the individual—of every race and creed—so that home would not be a strange or fearful place to those of us who return to claim the future, that future which belongs maybe not to us, but to our sons and daughters forevermore.

CPSIA information can be obtained
at www.ICGtesting.com
Printed in the USA
BVHW01s2218030918
526438BV00011B/219/P